THE HEALING DRUM

Yaya Diallo playing the djémé.

Photo by André Rival

THE HEALING DRUM

African Wisdom Teachings

YAYA DIALLO and MITCHELL HALL

Destiny Books
Rochester, Vermont

Destiny Books
One Park Street
Rochester, Vermont 05767

Library of Congress Cataloging-in-Publication Data
Diallo, Yaya.
The healing drum : African wisdom teachings / by Yaya Diallo and Mitchell Hall.
p.   cm.
Includes index.
ISBN 0-89281-256-7
1. Minianka (African people)—Mali—Music—History and criticism.
2. Folk music—Mali—History and criticism.   3. Music, Influence of.
4. Ritual—Therapeutic use.   I. Hall, Mitchell.   II. Title.
ML3760.D52   1989
781.766'23—dc19   89-1594
                                                                CIP
                                                                MN

Printed and bound in the United States

10 9 8 7 6 5

Destiny Books is a division of Inner Traditions International

Distributed to the book trade in Canada by
Publishers Group West (PGW), Toronto, Ontario
Distributed to the book trade in the United Kingdom by
Deep Books, London
Distributed to the book trade in Australia by
Millennium Books, Newtown, N. S. W.
Distributed to the book trade in New Zealand by
Tandem Press, Auckland
Distributed to the book trade in South Africa by
Alternative Books, Randburg

CONTENTS

Preface and Acknowledgments, vii

PART ONE: THOSE WHO REFUSE THE MASTER, 1

      Introduction, 3
      MITCHELL HALL
  1 Birth of a Fool, 13
  2 Family Life, 25
  3 Village Life, 37
  4 The Elders, 44
  5 Knowledge, 52
  6 Initiations and Secret Societies, 64

PART TWO: THE HEALING DRUM, 77

      Introduction, 79
      MITCHELL HALL
  7 Musical Instruments, 86
  8 The Minianka Musician's Apprenticeship, 95

CONTENTS

9   Music, Work, and Dance, 105

10   School, 119

11   Rituals and Celebrations, 129

12   Music and Healing, 141

13   Two Cultures, 172

14   The Healing Drum Today, 193

Pronunciation Key and Glossary of Minianka Terms, 201

Selected Bibliography, 205

Index, 207

About the Authors, 212

Audiocassette Ordering Information, 213

PREFACE AND
ACKNOWLEDGMENTS

The Healing Drum is a collaboration between the African musician, Yaya Diallo, and myself, an American writer. It tells the story of Yaya Diallo's life, of the culture of his tribe, the Minianka, and of the sacred, healing role of music in that culture.

My voice speaks in the introductions to each part of the book.

The rest of the book is in Yaya's voice. His narrative was created through a collaborative process. Over a period of seven months, he told me his stories, reflections, understandings, and concerns—in French. I transcribed and translated this material from the tape recordings of our conversations and, metaphorically speaking, set it to the music of written English.

To assure the authenticity and integrity of the story, I have striven to reflect faithfully Yaya Diallo's vision. I am grateful to my friend for trusting me to write and introduce his story, as well as for the joy I have experienced while listening and dancing to his music.

Managing editor Leslie Colket has been a supportive ally and constructive critic throughout the project. Editor Wendy Tilghman elicited enriching material from us through her perspicacious queries and gave invaluable assistance through her editorial and

PREFACE AND ACKNOWLEDGMENTS

organizational acumen. They are both thanked for their thoroughness, their care, their thoughtful dialogue, and their many contributions to strengthening the manuscript. Copy editor Joan Kocsis did an excellent, sensitive job.

To facilitate my writing, Ezra Hall, my son, initiated me into the skills of word processing and kindly lent me his computer. Rick Rayfield completed the set of needed hardware with the extended loan of a color monitor. Their material and moral support is much appreciated.

I thank my mother, Ruth, for teaching me to type on a manual typewriter when I was a young boy. As I have worked on the various drafts of this manuscript, I have gratefully remembered her foresight that typing was a skill I could always use. I also thank her for her ingenuous interest in verbal expression and for having supported the value that "books are your friends."

Katra Kindar, organizer of Compana Productions classes in African dance and drumming in Vermont, asked me to be Yaya Diallo's French-English interpreter. She was thus a link to our friendship, as was Sam Moffatt, Yaya's drumming student, who introduced him to Vermont.

Jared Cadwell, Green Mountain Valley School headmaster, and Doctor Richard Warmann of the Pleasant Chiropractic and Acupuncture Center in Montpelier, are both much appreciated for enthusiastically supporting my organizing of lecture-demonstrations for Yaya Diallo at their school and healing center respectively. While I interpreted for Yaya on these occasions, the idea for a book on his life and tradition became a vivid vision for me.

Larry Rice, national sales manager of Inner Traditions International, introduced me to the company and its editorial orientation in casual conversation at a seminar we both took together. My friends, Dr. Tony Stern and Larry Grinnell, both helped financially to make my participation in the seminar possible. All three men are thanked for linking me to this publishing company. Tony Stern, along with friends John Maybury and Dr. Catherine Roberts also encouraged me over the years to keep writing.

Publisher Ehud Sperling recognized the potential for this book and is appreciated for making it possible. His wife, Estella Arias, Inner Traditions art director, has ably overseen the design of the book.

During the period I have been writing *The Healing Drum,* classes

PREFACE AND ACKNOWLEDGMENTS

with dance teachers Arthur Hall, Richard Gonzalez, Pat Hall-Smith, and Beto Gadibem gave me opportunities to enjoy the vitality and appreciate the subtlety of African dance and drumming. Pat Hall-Smith, in particular, provided an occasion through her teaching when form, feeling, and meaning became one.

Thanks to my wife, Burgi, and our children—Ezra, Esme, Amela, Mireille, and Pierre—for accepting my need to spend long, solitary hours in my study working on this book.

Kwan Saihung and Deng Ming-Dao are thanked for their inspiring examples and helpful teaching.

Mitchell Hall

Warren, Vermont
March 1989

My gratitude toward two elders abides. Nangape Kone helped me through the most difficult trials in my village and in school. He gave me remedies to stabilize my inner being, and he protected me against any possible malevolent sorcery. Mansha Kone, in the presence of his children, washed me with a solution of protective plants to chase away any bad spirits that could have been there. He fought against the destructive forces of jealousy.

My mother has been the source of much good for me. I am fortunate to be learning from her still. At this stage of my life, my son Telli is of foremost importance to me. In the reincarnationist perspective of my tribe, he is my maternal grandfather who has returned through the union of a Spanish mother and an African father. In my home village of Fienso, he represents a hope. He is an intermediary between black and white people, as well as a recipient of the knowledge that the two cultures can contribute to each other. One day he could be a spokesperson for blacks and whites equally, as it has been predicted in the village.

My thanks to Sylvain Leroux, the flutest on my first album, *Nangape,* and to all the musicians with whom I worked on *The Healing Drum* audiocassette. My friend, Michel Bonneau of Montreal, is thanked for the photographs in this book and on *The Healing Drum* audiocassette. My thanks also to Helen Alemany for the book's cover art.

Yaya Diallo

Montreal
March 1989

PART ONE

THOSE
WHO REFUSE
THE MASTER

INTRODUCTION

Yaya **Diallo** is an African musician from the rural village of Fienso, in the Republic of Mali, in West Africa. He plays the vase-shaped hand drum known as the *djembe* and the *balafon,* which is like a wooden xylophone with gourd resonators. These are traditional instruments for many West African tribes, including Yaya's people, the Minianka.

Yaya Diallo began playing in his earliest years because of his own fascination with music, which was an integral part of village life. The musicians were not professionals but fellow villagers who also farmed, like everyone else. Music accompanied the rhythm of work in the fields by day just as it accompanied community dances in the village square at night. Music was an essential element of every marriage, initiation, ritual, and funeral.

The musicians were expected to maintain high moral standards because of their power to influence people through music. They were people of knowledge who were listened to carefully at village councils. In the Minianka expression, they spoke with *lafolo yati,* "the voice of the man who knows through the drum."

Two men in particular stand out in Yaya's reminiscences on the musicians of his youth. The first is his maternal grandfather, an accomplished musician and the traditional chief of the nearby village of Zangasso. The second man is Yaya's mentor and protector, the elder, seer, and musician, Nangape Kone. Nangape embodied a tribal ideal, the musician as healer. He combined virtuosity in drumming with profound understanding of human psychology, esoteric knowledge of the effects of sounds on humans and invisible spirits, proficiency in herbal medicine, involvement in rituals for the purification of the village and the individual, and sage simplicity. Yaya honored the memory of his teacher by naming his first record, released in 1980, *Nangape*.

In Minianka tradition, music serves a sacred, healing function for the individual and the society. A remedy for both physical and psychological imbalances, music facilitates communication with the ancestors, the spirits, and the Creator. Music harmonizes forces of the visible and invisible worlds. Yaya Diallo remains devoted to this path in his music.

Yaya was born in 1946. By that time, the French had already been politically, militarily, and economically controlling Yaya's part of Africa, which they called the French Sudan, for fifty-four years. In 1954, Yaya was enrolled in the French colonial school at Zangasso. From that time onward, his growing consciousness was exposed to two incompatible models of what human life should be. His own people educated him according to traditional Minianka values. His French teachers tried to undermine village influences, to make him and his classmates think and act like little Frenchmen. Great tensions resulted from these conflicting demands on his identity and cultural allegiance. Yaya was able to resolve those tensions in his life, but the process of individuation was not an easy one.

Yaya was a gifted and successful student. By the time he was in high school, Mali had become independent of France. Yaya was in the first class in the history of his high school to graduate with Malian rather than French diplomas. His government offered him a scholarship to begin studies in 1967 at the University of Montreal in Canada. He eventually graduated from the university with a Bachelor of Science degree in chemistry and worked for a few years in that field. Over time, he felt increasingly alienated from a laboratory career and heeded the call of the ancestral drum.

Yaya lives today in Montreal. He makes his living as a music teacher and performing musician. Employed by the music department of Carleton University in Ottawa to teach a course in aural training, he also gives workshops in hand drumming at various centers in North America.

Yaya is noted for being a demanding teacher. Because of his awareness of the impact of sounds on human well-being, he guides his students to play with an awakened consciousness about the effects of their music. He teaches his drumming students to listen, to observe, and to produce tones of the right quality. Yaya has found that it takes a devoted student a year of diligent practice to make the right sounds on the djembe, the sounds it was designed to make. Once that has been accomplished, he feels they are ready to go on and learn varied rhythms.

Yaya returns regularly to his home village of Fienso to visit with his family and to deepen his explorations of Minianka music and healing. The village elders are happy that he is pursuing a musical vocation based on the healing potential of music. Few of the young people are currently showing much interest in the traditional esoteric teachings. Modern Western culture with its technology, fashions, and electrically amplified music is alluring. The ancient, Minianka way of knowledge that has been transmitted only through oral tradition could be lost. How ironic it is, Yaya has observed, that at this moment when young Africans are discarding the drums in favor of Walkmen and electric guitars, growing numbers of Europeans and North Americans want to explore traditional African music.

Fienso and Montreal are worlds apart. In his youth, Yaya was nurtured by the culture of the drum. Now he lives in a culture dominated by television and other nonparticipatory forms of entertainment. By virtue of his background, the instruments and rhythms he plays, and his intention to bring joy to people through a quality of sound that promotes well-being, Yaya Diallo can be seen as a traditional Minianka musician. As a performer, he plays to audiences of diverse backgrounds combining balafon and violin, djembe, and saxophone, playing contemporary and traditional music, and is thus a pioneer of an emerging world music.

Africa is a vast and varied continent comprising 22 percent of the earth's land surface. It is the home of 11 percent of the world's human population. Over a thousand languages are spoken among these people, estimated in 1981 to number about 500 million. The subject of this book is one tradition among the many African cultures.

The country of Mali is in the geographical center of West Africa. To picture just where this is, imagine Africa as a revolver pointing south. Mali is approximately in the middle of the handle. It is landlocked, bordered by seven other countries: Algeria, Niger, Burkina Faso, Ivory Coast, Guinea, Senegal, and Mauritania.

The jigsaw-puzzle boundaries of Mali were cut by the French colonial rulers who established their domination over the region in 1892. In 1959, it went through a brief semiautonomous period when it was known as the Sudanese Republic. Then for two months in the summer of 1960, it joined with Senegal to form the short-lived Mali Federation, which foundered on political differences. The Republic of Mali became a political entity on September 22, 1960. The first independent government had a Marxist socialist orientation. In 1968 it was ousted by a military junta that suspended the constitution and outlawed political activity. In 1974, the military established a new constitution and a national assembly. There is only one legal political party today, the Democratic Union of the Malian People.

Mali was named after the gold-rich empire that ruled a large region around the headwaters of the Niger River from the thirteenth to the sixteenth centuries. This empire controlled plentiful gold and traded widely in ivory, ostrich feathers, salt, and slaves. The area where the Republic of Mali is today was a political, cultural, and commercial crossroads. It was the site of migrations and invasions of Berbers from the northwest, Jews from the northeast, and Arabs from the Arabian peninsula. Devastating warfare and slave raiding and trading were common, along with the vacillating fortunes of kingdoms and empires. The desert city of Timbuktu on the Niger River was not only a prosperous trading center in the Middle Ages, but also a sophisticated center of learning with its University of Sankore.

The opulence of some of the early empires contrasts with Mali's relative poverty today. Annual per capita income has been under $200 through the 1980s. The population was estimated in 1984 to be seven and a half million. The country is spread over 479,000 square miles, larger than the combined areas of Texas and California, yet only one percent of it is arable. Under normal conditions, with no drought, a quarter of the entire territory is suitable for pasture for such animals as cattle and goats.

The Malian climate is mostly hot and dry. The country is divided into three climatic zones. The southern sudanic zone of rolling plains—where Yaya grew up—receives the most rainfall, from 20 to 60 inches per year. Extending to 15° north latitude, it is an area of forest gallerics along the courses of rivers and wooded savanna lands. Among the common trees are mahogany, kapok, baobab, and several species largely unheard of in the West. The French planted the first mango trees in the western sudanic region, and since then the villagers have been planting them throughout the zone for their sweet and juicy fruit. Average temperatures range between 75° and 86° Fahrenheit. Wildlife once abounded here and still includes a multitude of birds, snakes, monkeys, crocodiles, hippopotami, giraffes, elephants, antelopes, gazelles, panthers, and lions.

Throughout Mali, the dry season is from November to June. Its first three months are cooled by a wind from the northeast called the *alize,* which brings temperatures down to a comfortable range around 70°. As the dry season progresses, the temperatures rise, and the last three months can be harshly hot. From February to June, the dry, dust-laden harmattan wind blows south from the Sahara. It is a trying time, with daily average temperatures over a 100° and higher incidences of health problems.

The rains arrive in June, with raucous thunderstorms and monsoon winds from the southwest. In July and August, heavy downpours can occur every few days, but they rarely last for more than a few hours. As crops are rainfed, the rainy season is also the season of intensive agricultural labor for the Malian peasants, who comprise about 90 percent of the population.

Millet is the staple grain cultivated by the Minianka. They grow three varieties of millet—large, small, and red. The first two are eaten, the third is fermented to make an alcoholic drink. A large, white, starchy tuber known as a yam, but quite different from the orange yams eaten in America, is a diet staple, especially when the stores of millet near their end and before the new crop is harvested. Rice is cultivated by the Minianka farmers and is the preferred dish to serve guests. Corn, manioc root, and potatoes are also grown.

THOSE WHO REFUSE THE MASTER

Throughout Africa's sudanic zone, the main dish of complex carbohydrates is served with a sauce that can include baobab leaves, bean plant leaves, and a vegetable oil made from peanuts, palm kernels, or other sources. Meat is eaten as it becomes available from hunting or from the sacrificial slaughter of animals such as chickens. Fish from the rivers is eaten fresh, dried, and smoked.

Fruits are abundant in the Minianka territory and include many kinds that are unknown in the West. One example is the *karite*. Its fruit is eaten, and its kernel provides an edible oil or butter that can also be turned into soap. The *zama* fruit is so plentiful that people can gather as much as they want. None of the trees have owners, and their produce is available to all. Mangoes, papayas, avocados, oranges, and grapefruit are among the other fruits cultivated by the Minianka.

Cotton exportation accounts for over 50 percent of Mali's foreign exchange currency. Minianka farmers in recent years have turned more and more to growing this crop for the money it can bring them.

Administratively, Mali has been divided by the government into 6 regions, 42 circles, and 286 arrondissements. The Minianka live principally in the southeastern circles of Koutiala and Yorosso. This is approximately the area between two rivers, the Bani, which is the major tributary of the mighty Niger river, and the Banifing. The Bani flows from southwest to northeast, the Banifing from east to west. The rivers separate the Minianka from the populous Bambara tribe to the north and west. The village of Fienso is in the circle of Koutiala and the arrondissement of Zangasso.

The Minianka are a subgroup of the Senufo tribe, who dwell in southeastern Mali, northern Ivory Coast, and northwestern Burkina Faso, comprising about two million people. No clear and hard lines distinguish the Minianka from the Senufo. Together they numbered about 434,000 in the late 1970s. One of the defining characteristics of the Minianka has been their refusal of all central authority. In fact, while the term Minianka is officially recognized today as the designation for Yaya's people, they do not refer to themselves by that name. They prefer to call themselves *Bamana,* which means "those who refuse the master." They resisted the external authority of the empires of the western sudan until the French conquest of the area in the 1890s. The final battle of that conquest was fought at the Senufo city of Sikasso, where, years later, Yaya Diallo attended high school.

One of the external authorities the Minianka have traditionally refused is the religion of Islam. In a country that is 65 percent Moslem and 5 percent Christian, most of the Minianka are among the remaining 30 percent of Malians who are animists. Like other animists, the Minianka believe that humans, the creatures and phenomena of nature, and invisible spirits are all endowed with souls. The Minianka worship one transcendent Creator, who is addressed through intermediary spiritual powers. Given the history of jihads—wars to enforce conversion to Islam—in the sudanic territory, it is not surprising that the decentralized Minianka pride themselves on having been fierce warriors. They could not have upheld their traditions without fighting to do so.

As "those who refuse the master," the Minianka villagers have often been perceived by authorities of the Malian government as recalcitrant traditionalists. The notion of central political authority is alien to Minianka culture. Even chiefs do not enjoy a higher standard of living or privileges of power over their fellows. In fact, "chief" is an inadequate translation of the Minianka term, which indicates a relationship of responsibility rather than power. The traditional Minianka chief* was above all a community peacemaker with ritual duties. The consent of the village council of elders and of village initiation societies was essential to his effective functioning.

Minianka decentralist tendencies extend to the spoken language. The French linguist, Jean Cauvin, distinguished seven dialects of the Minianka tongue in the area between the Bani and the Banifing. These dialects are situated within the wider Senufo context of—according to the claims of linguists—four distinct languages.

French is the official national language of the independent Republic of Mali. Although it is the language of the former colonial masters, in 1960 French was more acceptable to Mali's diverse tribes than one of their own languages because it did not give one tribe priority over the others. French was a much more widely spoken world language than any of the indigenous languages: books were more readily available in French, and the schools and

---

*For music to honor the traditional chief, listen to "Berete" on *The Healing Drum* audiocassette (see page 213 for ordering information).

civil service were already functioning through the medium of French. Speaking in French, Malians could communicate with Africans of other former French colonies. Schooled in French, Malian graduates could go on to learn needed skills at universities in Europe and Canada. Most other African states on the eve of their independence also solved the problem of choosing an official language in the same way and for similar reasons.

In the rural villages of Mali, of course, the tribal languages are still spoken, just as they were when Yaya was a boy. Fienso lies in a plain traversed by a large stream. To the north and the south are low mountains. With a stream flowing close by, the soundscape of Yaya's childhood was graced with the burbling of water, the calls of multicolored birds that frequented the banks, and at times the sounds of the swimming crocodiles. During the rainy season, he would hear the dripping of water onto his house, a round hut of mud bricks and a conical thatched roof. When he left the house to work in the fields near the northern mountains, he would be entertained by the calls of different species of birds, each with its distinctive tones and melodies. At night, the many cries of the wild sounded: the hyenas, panthers, and lions on the prowl, the cries of warthogs, monkeys, and what people said were invisible spirits.

Around the village at night strange lights appear that no one has been able to explain. Points of light float in the air, suddenly becoming very strong, shining on people's bodies, and going from tree to tree. Just as suddenly, they disappear, then reappear, and disappear again. The entire village is surrounded by these mobile, floating balls of light, appearing unpredictably. All who have encountered them report that the lights become increasingly bright and give off heat. Yaya often saw one behind his house at night.

Through communal projects, such as installing wells and maintaining roads, the villagers of Fienso have achieved a sense of unity. The village council has endeavored to make it possible for each family to support itself through its own labor and to be without debt to anyone else. Yet outsiders rarely immigrate to Fienso because they are unfamiliar with the village's many traditions and prohibitions and often afraid of the spirits believed to exist nearby. A Christian congregation attempted to establish itself in the village but was gone within a year; its church stands empty. A mosque has been more successful and has won some adherents to Islam.

INTRODUCTION

The Malian government recognizes Fienso as the source of an unusually large number of intellectuals. Out of a population of a thousand people, with no school closer than a seven-kilometer walk away, twenty natives have earned university diplomas in recent decades, including some doctors and engineers. No one knows why the level of intelligence in the village is high, but it is naturally another source of local pride. They see that in the context of the educational system of the white civilization, they have produced capable children. Many other Malian villages with schools have fewer than two university graduates.

Among all the myths and folklore of the Senufo, there are no stories of migrations. The Senufo claim to have always dwelt where they are now. Remarkably, they have never been made part of any of the empires that extended over large nearby areas. Their rich and detailed oral tradition does not include the names of the emperors who imposed their wills on numerous other tribes. Only by way of the national radio station does such history reach the village of Fienso.

The Minianka of Fienso and other villages pride themselves on being highly initiated into the mysteries of traditional animism. When they hear of the glories of past black Islamic empires of Mali, the Minianka have no desire to appropriate that history as part of their own heritage. Their ancestors had never ventured into colonial or imperial expansion, but, to the shame of some today, they had engaged in slave trading.

Whereas the Minianka have not migrated within living memory, in the rare instances when other peoples came to their area, the immigrants were accommodated or assimilated. Yaya's paternal great-grandfather—the Fulani herder who stopped to nurse a sick cow and subsequently married a Minianka—is a case in point. The Fulani are a nomadic, cattle-herding people scattered widely over the entire savanna region of West Africa. Some of the Fulani mixed with other tribes, became sedentarized, and combined agriculture with their cattle herding. Yaya's father, born of the Fulani-Minianka lineage, carried the Fulani family name, Diallo, and continued the cattle-herding vocation. Like his father, Yaya maintained a sort of Fulani identity while at the same time participating fully in the Minianka culture, going through the initiations and rituals appropriate to his age group.

In this countryside of baobab and fromager trees, of sacred

groves and poisonous serpents, of grassy plains and sandstone plateaus, Yaya learned through rich experience and painful apprenticeship to adapt himself to a world that was not always hospitable. When he returns to the village now, it takes him about a week to feel at ease and confident that he will not unwittingly violate any of the taboos. He also needs a week to adjust to the profound darkness at night, so different from the atmosphere of our illuminated North American cities.

When Yaya visits Fienso, he is especially concerned with the youth of the village. They are aware that he lives in Montreal, and that he has seen such cities as New York and Paris. Consequently, his playing of the hand drums and balafon is seen by the youth as a strong affirmation of the enduring value of their traditional culture and its music. He plays in some ceremonies when he is back in Mali, but he does not have the time for the lengthy ritual purifications and abstinences that would allow him to participate in others. He is often content to sit with the other adults and discuss how to pass on the tribal heritage to the new generations. The present population of the Minianka villages, as of Mali in general, is predominantly young. Over 50 percent of Malians, in fact, are under fifteen years of age. Because the youth are attracted to many popular Western influences, transmitting the traditional Minianka culture to them is a complex challenge.

When Yaya has brought Canadians and Americans to Fienso, the village elders have recognized this as supportive of the traditional ways, for these Westerners have been eager to learn about drumming and village life. Unlike the earlier white colonialists who wanted to destroy the African culture, the new visitors affirm it through their respect and interest. Yaya comments on this phenomenon with a touch of irony, "The West may help preserve African culture for the Africans."

BIRTH
OF A FOOL

The fool is content to be himself, to be what he is today. He has ceased dreaming of what he ought to be and will never be. I am a fool who is healing. In Africa, when a fool is healed, he is called a former fool. So, having been a fool, I will always find this term attached to my name. My musical training brought me back onto the path of healing.

There have been accidents in my life. When I describe what I have lived through, people think it is a fable. If I had planned my life, I would have missed my destiny. I could not have foreseen so many unexpected occurrences, so many paradoxes!

My story begins thus. I was born of a foolish union: I am a Fulani-Minianka. That sounds bizarre to the ears of people who know these tribes. The probability that a Fulani man would meet a Minianka woman, marry her, and settle down was once zero; the nomadic life of the Fulani herders is so different from the ways of the sedentary Minianka.

It was a sick cow that caused my Fulani ancestor to stop one day in Fienso. The cow lay down. The man said, "As long as that cow does not move, I am not moving." He stayed to care for it, but the cow still did not get up. Meanwhile, he saw a young Minianka woman walk by on the way to get some water. They spoke. Soon thereafter they decided to marry. He was my great-grandfather. A family of Fienso adopted him right away and showed him the ways of the Minianka. The brothers of my great-grandfather continued their nomadic search for fresh pasture and settled elsewhere.

I was born into a family in which my father was the oldest of three brothers. There had been a fourth, but he left, and three remained. Among the brothers, there was only hatred, caused by rivalry over the inheritance and who was going to have the first child. In our family, Fulani and Minianka notions about inheritance were mixed. In the hierarchy of my family, the eldest of each generation directs everything.

According to Fulani tradition, when a child is born, he is given a heifer. When the heifer is older, she will reproduce. By the time the young Fulani has reached the age of twenty-one, he has his own herd and can depart to be on his own. When the father dies, his herd is divided among his sons.

Despite this tradition, our family kept the Minianka structure, in which the eldest boy of the new generation manages the entire herd. This resulted in intense rivalry among the brothers as to who would have the first son. That was the beginning of the hatred. It affected the women also, for the one to have the oldest son would be the mistress of the compound with all attendant privileges. She would keep the gold and control the milk and all other things.

My mother came from a Minianka family of traditional and administrative chiefs of Zangasso, a village two miles away from my native Fienso. Her father was chief in the village, a fine musician, a hunter, an initiator, an elder responsible for the rituals of initiation, and a healer. Music was important to him. As chief, every Friday morning he received and listened to only the best of musicians and singers. It was said that anyone who sang poorly at these sessions would be whipped. But the singing was always good. As a boy, I often stayed in my maternal grandmother's hut in Zangasso and was awakened on Friday mornings by this excellent music.

My maternal heritage represented all the best of Africa. Although my mother never became rich in material possessions, she had no cause to envy a wealthy, Islamic lady with golden earrings. Her gold is within her, it is her human heritage. In her childhood, she had known her father as a man who stood on his own feet, who was initiated into all the secret societies possible, who had knowledge and used it wisely.

Prophecy

My maternal grandmother tells the story that when she was carrying my mother on her back, three elders saw the baby and said that wherever this girl went in later life, she would be seen as a sorceress. This meant she was born with a gift that would make her more perceptive than the average person, more deeply concerned with values, more powerful. Fearing her power, others would confuse it with sorcery despite her good purposes.

Later the elders told my mother that she would give birth to a child who would become a person of much knowledge, who would never go unnoticed wherever he was in the world. When she married and began to have children, she wondered with each new birth whether this was the one about whom the elders had spoken.

When she was pregnant with me, one elder told her the child she carried might be the one awaited in the family, and it would go through extraordinary experiences to make its greatness.

"As his mother," the elder forewarned, "you will have to withstand all the pains he will suffer. No one will be able to destroy him through pain. No wickedness will ever stop him."

I was born in my paternal grandmother's house in Fienso. She was the midwife who assisted all the births in our village and to whom women from several surrounding villages came for help. I was born so quickly there was no time for the usual preparations, or for the customary attendance of the older women. My mother said she felt no pain, just a mild pressure, and there I was.

My grandmother looked at my newborn face and said, "Oh no, not him!"

She recognized me as an ancestor returned to earth. This does not disturb me. I accept this double role of being both myself and an ancestor at the same time.

The Minianka do not consider human beings and the visible plant and animal species to be the only inhabitants of the earth. Through their own invisible dimensions, humans are in contact with other beings and forces in the invisible realms. The ancestors occupy an important place there.

THOSE WHO REFUSE THE MASTER

Although they have left the world physically, the ancestors dwell close to the living, and can provide guidance in following the customs correctly. Their world is conceived as identical in structure to that of the living. There are circles of ancestors with their own sociology. When a person dies, he or she encounters these ancestral circles and hopes to be integrated into them. Acceptance into the community of the ancestors depends upon having lived a good life. Since ancestors can be reborn into the family, their interaction with the living is very direct. If they judge a woman wicked, they can make her sterile. If they deem her to have atoned, they can render her fertile. There is a coming and going between the visible and invisible worlds.

While I was still a tiny infant, an elder came with a present for my mother—a stick. He had prepared this stick in an occult way to enable my mother to deal with me in the difficult moments he foresaw to lie ahead with me. When I rebelled, only my mother's magic stick could restore me to calm and sensible behavior. Often she had only to touch me with it, but when she was beside herself, she sometimes forgot the more subtle effects of the stick and landed solid blows on my body. Now I laugh in remembering these things, but they were not so funny at the time.

The prophecy that I would go through hardships to become a great person never led my mother to expect a rich son. To her, greatness implied someone who would be knowledgeable and who could bring order and harmony to a group of people. But I never felt any pressure from her to fulfill a special role. In fact, I do not claim to be the one who was prophesied. Only when I returned to the village after I had become a chemist did she confide her earliest hopes for me.

While growing up, I forgot about the predictions. I had no reason to suspect that the knowledgeable person foretold for the family could be me. To the contrary, my uncles repeatedly gave me the message that I was stupid, and this made a more immediate impression on me.

Human greatness is measured by the difficulties through which a person passes while remaining standing. To fall and stand again is a necessary condition of growing up. In our culture, suffering is not considered necessarily bad. It comes inevitably with life, and we were taught that life is not a gift. The world is not a comfortable living room in which we can simply sit in pleasant conversation;

we need to make efforts. Moreover, the African climate does not allow laziness. If we do not learn at home to exert ourselves physically and mentally, nature will be hard on us. If we do not accept suffering along the way, we will be unreconciled to life.

I cannot count how many times I was walking in the bush and was attacked by wasps, which stung me repeatedly on the head. As a child, of course, I cried from the pain, but it passed. It is certain that such things will happen to us. We need the inner assurance that we can meet them and not be shaken.

Death also must be confronted. One can be walking with a friend along a narrow path in the bush when a small serpent suddenly strikes, and the friend falls mortally wounded. One needs the strength of character to overcome such losses. For the African, life is short and precarious. We have not been able to eliminate snakes and scorpions from our environment; they creep around even in our cities.

Fienso

Fienso means in Senufo, "the village that will always exist." A center of deep tradition and knowledge, it is known for its autonomy and independence, for the dignity and hard work of its people. Local pride is strong.

In the past, Fienso was renowned and feared for producing fierce and unpitying warriors. It is also famed for its highly skilled musicians and healers. The Malian government recognizes Fienso as one of the villages that has given the largest number of intellectuals to the country despite the village's 90 percent illiteracy rate.

Fienso also has numerous sites with prohibitions attached to them. These places arouse fear in some of the inhabitants. There are well-known and widespread stories of the numerous spirits said to exist in the vicinity. In the middle of the village is a sacred wood where it is forbidden to enter with any metal that might cut a tree. Nearby is another thicket where one may not throw any objects or enter at all. At still another site, it is prohibited to call anyone at noon. There are other places in the village with peculiar taboos, such as not being allowed to sit down at a certain time of day. When I used to hear villagers from other areas speak of my village, I wondered how it was I could live there, and I was sometimes afraid to return home.

THOSE WHO REFUSE THE MASTER

Figure 1. Thatched huts provide temporary shelter beside a farmer's fields outside of Fienso.

When I was growing up, Fienso was composed of four neighborhoods. Their names in our language translate as the big neighborhood, the elephant's neighborhood, the neighborhood where they are well grounded, and the foreigner's neighborhood. I dwelt in the third of these. As we were situated between the first two, the name of our section of the village implied we were not to disturb our neighbors to either side. The first family to have settled in the village had its own section, and *Kle-Goa*, the house dedicated to the creator God, was located there.

The village was wooded, with many large trees. Baobabs, the elephants of the tree family, with their trunks 20 meters in circumference, stood their ground and provided shade. There were also the almost equally large fromager trees, which provided kapok from their pods, the fiber used for stuffing pillows and mattresses.

When I was a boy, our earthen huts were round and arranged in roughly circular fashion in compounds. The doors of each hut faced the center of the compound, where the cooking was done. Today, square and rectangular dwellings have become popular. Still fashioned of earth, they are squared off more in the Islamic style.

The village square was in our neighborhood, shaded by great

Figure 2. Flat-topped huts and thatched roof granaries of present day Fienso.

trees, frequented by the elders of our village council by day, the scene of our community dances by night. Another square, the place of the dead, was near the edge of the village. In this place, villagers set down a recently deceased body to dance and sing farewell before carrying it outside the village to the cemetery. This was a corner of the village that, as a boy, I would avoid going to late at night.

If you were to ask the chief of a Minianka village such as Fienso the size of the population of his village, he would be embarrassed. He would not know how to determine the extent of the visible world or the limits of the invisible. How far does the village extend? Where are the boundaries of the two worlds? Every day, the invisible and visible parts of the world border, intersect, and mutually influence each other. Likewise, notions of ethnic group or nation are fuzzy; it is difficult to speak of them as such.

My village is composed of fifty extended families. Each family may have forty members. Among them, ten family names are used. Each family dwells in large compounds, which include individual huts and the round granaries where millet, rice, and corn are stored. Food is prepared for the entire family outside in a communal kitchen within each compound. Alongside the kitchen in a prominent place is a large stone called the stone of the ancestors.

Stone of the Ancestors

When a family comes to settle somewhere, this stone is the first object placed at the new homesite. It symbolizes unity and reminds family members of humility, of freedom from greed, and of their descent from the ancestors. The sense of coming from a defined, meaningful past is important. A portion of food is left daily by the stone of the ancestors with the understanding that these departed spirits will come in the night to sit on the stone and partake of the food. This food offering can also be seen as an expression of gratitude to preceding generations who have provided a place to live and a viable lifestyle. Annually, the sacrifice of a chicken is made to the stone of the ancestors. This is a way of recognizing all that the stone of the ancestors represents.

One also sees in the kitchen the fire, large clay pots, calabashes that serve as bowls, mortars carved out of tree trunks, and pestles bigger than baseball bats. Two or three women may stand around a mortar and rhythmically pound the grain until it is ready for the cooking pot over the fire.

Each family compound has two gates. The public gate, oriented to the west, is used for daily comings and goings. The gate of the ancestors, oriented to the east, is reserved for special occasions such as leaving the village for a long voyage. When someone dies in the compound, the body is carried out through the gate of the ancestors. When a baby is born, the placenta is buried next to this gate.

The Sacred Wood

What is most characteristic of Fienso and all Minianka villages is the sacred wood. This is a small forest or grove, in the middle of which is a special tree called the firstborn. The Minianka say that the trees and plants have their ancestors, just as human beings do. The firstborn is considered the first plant that Kle, the Creator God, created and thus the ancestor of all other plants. Only the most highly initiated know which it is so that it may be all the more protected through secrecy. The entire grove is a sanctuary for the firstborn tree, and no one has the right to cut any of the trees in the sacred wood.

In some villages like Fienso no one may even enter the sacred wood if they have any metal or matches on them. Some say that evil spirits are sheltered in the wood, and therefore it is unwise to venture there at just any moment of the day. If someone were found with a fire in the sacred wood, this would be a sacrilege and would lead to severe consequences. If the sacred wood burns, it is considered an omen of misfortune for the community. In case of catastrophe, all efforts would be made to save the first-born tree so that, in its role as ancestor of all other plants and trees, it could propagate vegetation again. Cultivating a great respect for nature is the ultimate goal of all the customs concerning the sacred wood.

As a boy, in April 1958, I completely burned down the sacred wood of Zangasso, the birthplace of my mother, where my grandparents lived. Customarily, at a precise date each year, the elders clear the ground in the sacred grove of any grass or plants. This practice prevents fire from spreading rapidly so that the ancestral tree could be saved. It is also a celebration in honor of the sacred wood. It is said that if this celebration does not take place, the rains will not fall. During the year in question, the elders had been negligent. A new chief had been entitled, and in the changeover of authority the village elders completely forgot the date for the ritual clearing.

I was walking along barefoot by the sacred wood of Zangasso when a snake suddenly struck out at me. I leaped out of the way, and the serpent barely grazed my foot. As the grass was tall and dry, I was not able to pursue the snake to kill it. I called out to it as it retreated through the grass, "You missed me, snake, but I am not going to miss you." I ran to get a glowing ember from a nearby fire and with it set the grass on fire, to smoke out the snake.

The grass was so dry that the fire spread rapidly in spite of the villagers' efforts to douse the flames with water from their homes.

"Who set this fire?" people asked.

"Yaya did; he's sitting over here."

To repair the damage, seven bulls would have to be sacrificed, and the villagers would have to go to another site to find a suitable firstborn tree to transplant to Zangasso. My father was supposed to provide the seven bulls from his herd to save my life; otherwise, I would have to be sacrificed in a few short days. My father, however, declared, "Kill him; let him die." I sat there thinking that perhaps I would die.

The harshness of my father's reaction is mitigated by the fact that in his Fulani tradition the cattle of his herd are his raison d'être. The words of one song state, "If you think a Fulani is cowardly, walk into his herd and see what he will do to you." I remember times when a cow and a child were sick at the same time—my father went to care for the cow first. To his mind, the price of seven bulls was extremely steep. Furthermore, since he was not one hundred percent Minianka, he had reservations about the importance of the sacred wood. One cow would have been too much for him to pay for something in which he did not believe.

I understood his reaction right away, as I had been raised to appreciate the importance of cattle in the herding culture. Naturally, cows were not worth more than a human life, but he would not give any. Even today, if he had to choose between giving up one of his cows or going to prison, he would prefer the latter alternative. He felt at the time that if he surrendered the seven bulls, this would set a risky precedent that others would have abused. Each time one of his children had committed some mischief, cows could have been demanded of him. Perhaps even the villagers would have taken his cattle for annual sacrifices. So he stood firmly against the price demanded of him.

The entire matter would have to be decided by the village council of elders. Finally, I was summoned to them. When I arrived, I saw the elders' trembling. The fire was not deemed to be my fault; the reasoning was subtle. First of all, my role in relation to the ancestors was taken into account. While my mother came from Zangasso, where I set the fire, my father was from the village of Fienso. Upon marriage, following the patrilineal custom, my mother left Zangasso to dwell with my father in Fienso, where I was born. By virtue of my ancestry, I am the intermediary of the ancestors of Zangasso toward the ancestors of Fienso. Consequently, in my mother's original village, no one may harm me, not even the sorcerors. Furthermore, the elders confessed in their verdict, "We have failed in our duty. The day when we were supposed to clean around the wood has passed. We are three weeks late for the annual celebration. Our ancestors have made use of their intermediary to refresh our memories."

The entire village of Zangasso was then assessed to pay for the bulls that would be sacrificed for what the elders judged to be a double crime. The first crime was neglect of the cleaning ceremony around the wood, which led to the fire. The second was having reprimanded and frightened me, the intermediary of the ancestors, whose pardon would be asked for both offenses. Thus, my life was saved. Another ancestral tree was found and transplanted to Zangasso to reestablish the sacred grove there. The villagers became more vigilant in observing the rituals after this incident, at least for a time.

In the 1970s, another incident occurred at Zangasso that again reminded the people of the importance of the sacred wood. The villagers decided to convert to Islam and no longer to believe in "those things," that is, the traditional observances.

Zangasso was susceptible to Islamization partly because of its location. The government built a road that passes next to the village, and so Moslem immigrants from the drought-stricken north of Mali had easy access to Zangasso, and many settled there. An Islamic quarter grew and increasingly influenced village life. The young people especially went back and forth between the two sections of the village. As Islam is a proselytizing religion, and as Moslems are the majority of the Malian population, the pressures on the animists to convert were strong. Zangasso is not the only village in the Minianka region to be affected in this way; the Islamic influence is spreading.

As a result of their conversion to Islam, the villagers of Zangasso cut down their sacred wood, the very one that I had burnt. What was once so bushy and full of vines and creepers was transformed into a clearing, and the annual celebration in honor of the sacred wood was abolished.

What happened? The rains ceased. Famine began. During the dry season of the year after the wood was cut, the young people of the village saw black rain clouds forming and moving in the direction of Zangasso. Then suddenly the clouds swerved to avoid the village and went on to pour upon the neighboring villages, but not upon Zangasso.

According to another story, a sorceress sent lightning to strike a hut in which there were seven men. "If the first born tree were here, that would not have happened," said some of the people. After a year, the celebration of the sacred wood was reinstituted. Some years later, though, the area remained a clearing. "The firstborn tree is dead," the people said. Although an attempt was made to replant the firstborn tree, the wood never flourished again.

The Natural World

The wide variety of plants and trees and animal species are all honored and respected by the Minianka. Humans are directly related to the plants as well as to the animals through family history or through various initiations. This is acknowledged by different taboos and ceremonies. For example, because I am part Fulani, I can never eat monkey since all Fulani feel a special alliance with the monkey.

Water, like the people, animals, and plants, has its own history. It is the vital principle. Next to the village of Fienso, there is a pocket in the riverbed considered to be the source of all the water. No foreign water can be mixed in with this water. In case of drought, this water will save the people, as the spirit of conservation of water is there. The link between the people and this ancestral water is upheld each year in an important ceremony performed by only the most qualified members of the community. The people are called to respect this water and to entreat it not to abandon them.

As animists, the Minianka perceive a spirit in everything that surrounds them. These spirits do not take the place of God, although they are acknowledged for their rightful role in the orchestration of all creation. Pebbles, stones, rocks, mountains, the earth itself, all have special meaning to the Minianka. Stones exemplify the important virtue of humility to us. Even the air, which animates all things in the environment, is respected. For a long time my people have practiced conservation of the forests, water, and earth. We recognize our interdependence with all parts of the cosmos.

Rituals are acknowledgments that without the support of every aspect of the environment, we cannot live. One cannot disturb any element of nature without upsetting the rest. Thus, all humans are obliged to observe the fundamental rules of knowing how to live in proper relationship with all that is.

2

FAMILY LIFE

For my people, the social structure must be a support to living in harmony with the cosmos, and the family, known as *bouu* in Minianka, is clearly the most important subgroup of the community. It is so extended that the youth most often do not know how many people it includes. The family is composed of the ancestors, grandparents, parents, uncles, aunts, and, in a wider sense, the entire ethnic group.

If we conceive of the extended Minianka family as a great circle, within it are several smaller circles. First of all is the circle of the ancestors. Although not physically present, they nonetheless influence the life of the earth dwellers. They have preceded the living and established customs and knowledge. They watch over the respect for morality and decide who is to be born on earth. They reward or punish all acts and are the intermediaries between the Creator, Kle, and their living descendants. In the Minianka's patrilineal system, it is taught that all members of the family are descended from the same ancestor, like the Western family tree. It gives a sense of belonging to something in common.

The circle of the elders or adult males comes after the ancestors.

THOSE WHO REFUSE THE MASTER

In the case of my family, it consists of my father and three uncles, or my "four fathers," as I will explain below. They have received the ancestral education and must teach it impartially to all the children. The oldest of the men, my father, is the head of the family. He directs the ceremonies for worship of the ancestors and coordinates all activities. He keeps vigil over family harmony and manages the material and spiritual patrimony of his lineage. Among the relatives, the oldest is accorded respect, but he also respects the others.

The circle of women, also called the circle of mothers, in my family, is the wives of the four brothers. All of the women have the right to discipline any of the children. Hierarchy among them does not depend on age but rather on how long each has been in her husband's household. Thus, each time a new wife enters the family, the wife with seniority is relieved of some of her chores. Thanks to this system, my mother no longer works in the fields or in the kitchen. She takes care of the family's children.

Each individual has several "mothers" and "fathers"—the words uncle and aunt do not exist in the language. Likewise, one has many grandparents. When my son, Telli, visited the village of Fienso for the first time at the age of seven, he was so overwhelmed with all of these relatives that he exclaimed, "I have ten thousand grandfathers!"

The word for father, *n'tio*, can be confusing since it has three connotations. In its proper sense, it refers to the husband of the woman who has given birth to the child. Figuratively, it means the brothers of the father in the Western sense. More communally, n'tio stands for each man who is the same age as the husband of the woman who gave birth to the child. To make matters still more complex, a person can even be older than his father. For example, during his visit to Fienso, Telli was carrying a little baby on his back. The little one defecated on him. Telli told me he wanted to slap the baby.

"You mustn't hit him," I answered, "he is your father."

Naturally, Telli could not understand this concept. Since the baby's mother had by marriage become one of my "mothers," her son, although just an infant, had the same generational status as me and was therefore Telli's "father." There is a comical aspect to this that is not missed by the Minianka. Additionally, as there is no word for teacher in the language, the person who plays that role is also conceived of as a father.

As can be inferred, the word for mother, *Nou,* also has a comparable range of connotations. Mother refers to the woman who gave birth to the child, to her husband's other wives, to the members of her age group, and to an adult woman mentor or wife of a mentor. The mother is the foremost educator.* The elders assert, "When you educate a boy, you educate an individual, but when you educate a girl, you educate a family." The mother is the child's first teacher. She is the preserver of tradition par excellence. She directs family activities. Her domain is the kitchen, and the man does not have the right to set foot in it. In case of such an infraction, he can even be called before the family or village council or become the laughing stock of his age group.

At the time of marriage, the woman leaves her home to live with her husband in his home. The children will bear his family name. Other subgroups of the Senufo are matrilineal. In them, the husband leaves his family of origin to live with his wife's family, and the children carry on their mother's family name. Often the maternal uncle plays a key role in raising these children. The two systems, matrilineal and patrilineal, are similar. Sometimes there may even be a mixed marriage, where the husband and wife come from the two backgrounds and find a viable solution for their own ongoing family lineage. The children of a marriage inherit certain taboos, totems, and relationships to fetishes through either the father's or the mother's line depending on the system.

Marriage, or *fourou,* is the union of two families or two villages or two ethnic groups through the intermediary of two individuals. Its basis is not attraction to physical beauty alone; one marries to procreate. To the Minianka, the most beautiful woman is the one who carries a small child on her back.

If a couple has been married for two years, and no child results from the union, they may be subject to comments like, "What is going on there? Are you sleeping in the same bed?" The assumption is then made that the wife is sterile. Polygamy may sometimes be the result. The wife may suggest to her husband that he take

---

*For music to honor the feminine nurturing principle, listen to "Niere Yago" on *The Healing Drum* audiocassette (see page 213 for ordering information).

another wife, as the continuance of the family is felt to be very important. "I have not come here to close a family," she will say. If the second wife also fails to become pregnant, then most likely the husband is the sterile partner, and divorce may follow. High priority is given to the propagation of family lines.

On a recent trip to Fienso, I arrived in the middle of a tragic situation that illustrates this. One of my mothers, or aunts, had married an only child. This couple in turn produced only one son. A theft occurred, a serious offense to the Minianka. Procedures were carried out to discover the thief. To defend the innocence of his son, my aunt's husband and his father declared that whoever had committed the theft should die. It turned out his son was guilty, and the boy died. The mother became very disturbed, not only because of the loss of her son, but also because she felt responsible for the ending of a branch of the human family.

Since marriage is understood to bring together not just the two individuals but whole families at the very least, divorce is extremely complex among the Minianka. When children are born from the marriage, they are the living links between the two groups. Thus, even though the parents may separate, the marriage, in the sense of the union between the two families, remains intact. The existence of the children implies deep roots and bears the promise of the ancestral past. The children cannot be cut off from the families that have given rise to them. Marriage then is a serious matter.

If a husband is sterile, and his wife conceives a child through an adulterous relationship, that child belongs to the husband's family, not to that of the biological father. The child can never inherit anything from the biological father. In village life, a child conceived in this way may well resemble his father and know who the father is, given the smallness of the community. Such a situation can lead to psychological difficulties that are not easily resolved, as they are intertwined with sociological conditions.

The child, or *n'pia*, is considered the extension of the community. Birth is viewed as the return of an ancestor who had departed for a long voyage, and yet each child is welcomed as a unique being with specific roles to play in the community. Childish mistakes are not seen as incorrigible. Children are allowed the errors to be expected of their stage of development, but they must outgrow them. What is acceptable at one stage of life is unacceptable at another.

FAMILY LIFE

Within the circle of children, all are treated as equals. The older ones nonetheless help in caring for the younger ones and exercise some authority over them. The children create among themselves relations of unimaginable solidarity, complicity, and belonging. They eat together from the same plate. When the youngest have satisfied their hunger, then the oldest eat the rest. The oldest child of the family can give orders to his brothers and sisters, yet he has many duties to his younger siblings. For example, if he buys a watch, it does not belong to him alone. A brother who would like to use it does not need to wait for his permission to borrow it. Besides the authority of the eldest, none of the children in the family has any special privileges. All children wear the same color clothes sewn into the same design; they do not have any choice in the matter. By giving the same thing to each child, the adults avoid complaints that would disturb family harmony.

N'bade means a brother or sister from the same biological mother. This word evokes profound feelings of affection, as the children of the same mother bond strongly and positively with one another. By contrast, *n'fade* refers to a brother or sister of the same father but a different mother. A mutual dislike for one another is characteristic of children related in this way. The competition among them is serious and complicated by hatred, jealousy, ill wishes, and challenges. If a Minianka speaks of his *n'fade*, he implies that he does not expect any affection from that relative. If he becomes mentally unbalanced, he suspects that a curse has been sent by an uncle, that is, by an *n'fade* of his father or mother. Even failure on an examination will be thus explained. As my own experience bears out, poisonings are most likely done by someone from within the family, not by an outsider who is a declared enemy. The latter will keep his distance.

Customs

A foreigner, or *nampou*,[*] who visits or settles among the Minianka, is evaluated by other villagers according to the character and reputation of the local host. If the foreigner is received by a family of poorly behaved, ill-reputed Minianka, then the foreigner will not

---

[*]For music honoring the role of foreigners, listen to "Nampou" on *The Healing Drum* audiocassette (see page 213 for ordering information).

be held in high esteem. A nampou can expect a warm welcome from the villagers to the extent that his or her hosts are honored in the community. It has happened that a woman from another tribe or country marries a Minianka and goes to live in his village. If she feels isolated there and is not accepted by the community, it is not because of xenophobia but rather because her husband is mistrusted by the neighbors. Naturally then, they will be suspicious of her. Circumstances like this have been the source of much social disturbance. The only protection against this is to know the moral character of one's local hosts through inquiry and circumspection.

When one is a guest of the Minianka, the rules of courtesy require that one offer gifts of smoking tobacco, called *sara*. Among other tribes, kola nuts serve the same ritual function. Each newly married groom must distribute chewing tobacco to the community. A foreigner's first gesture of politeness after the customary greetings is to offer a bit of tobacco to the host. No one is obliged to actually use the tobacco, but offering and receiving it show proper upbringing.

There is a season for holidays and celebrations that goes from December to May, the dry season. A holiday is known as *kata*. This is the period of the year for meeting, sitting together, speaking, drinking, eating plentifully, playing and dancing, honoring the sacred wood and the ancestors, performing the funerals of those who died during the agricultural season from May to November.

Soume, an alcoholic drink derived from honey, is the most popular drink the Minianka serve at celebrations. Soume is drunk out of calabashes and it is said that around the calabash the young can learn of secret things. For when the old people drink, they loosen up and want to share who they are with the young. "Hey, little one, do you see me? Do you know who I am and what I know? Those people over there are imbeciles. They don't know me. Do you see that tree over there? You take a certain part of it, and if a snake bites you, the plant will be your remedy. The snakebite will be no more consequential than a fly bite."

When the old people brag around the calabash, they share valuable knowledge. I learned many things from my mother in this way. Nonetheless, alcoholism is also a problem among the Minianka just as it is here. Provided it is not abused, soume is a source of much constructive socializing. Sometimes a woman will serve her friends the drink she has brewed at home. They will share in it and sing together. Then they will wander to another's house and continue singing into the night around the calabash. Minianka babies get used to such nocturnal revelries and learn to sleep through the noise.

Tien

The Minianka have a word, borrowed from the Bambara people, that means inheritance. The word is *tien*. It is what the ancestors have left to their descendants. In its nonmaterial aspect, it can include a profession, a name, a prohibition, or a taboo. One will hear people say, "To be a farmer is my inheritance." In its material aspect, tien is the greatest source of disruption in the Minianka society.

At the death of the head of the family, his material possessions are not divided and shared among family members. The eldest of all the male children, whether or not he is intelligent, is the heir who will manage all the goods that had belonged to his father. Consequently, often each male child would like to occupy the position of eldest. The tension among the women in the household can be severe. The one who gave birth to the eldest boy is enviously regarded by the others. They may fear that the power of managing the inheritance will be abused. This happened in the case of my mother.

My mother's difficulties with her new family began at her marriage. My father was required to pay the bride price to my mother's parents, which was a cow that happened to be the last of his family's herd. My mother was reproached for this, even though such a tribute to the in-laws was customary.

She then had the bad luck of being the first woman among the three wives of the three brothers to give birth to a child, and her difficulties with her new family became magnified. This brought a great deal of jealousy against her. All the siblings who preceded me died under suspicious circumstances.

I lost an older brother in terrible circumstances that are unclear, but we know it was a murder. I also lost an older sister, whom I knew: one day she went to the well and fell in, to her death. It was not just an accident. Soon after me, a sister and brother were born. My little brother was murdered, too. We do not know who threw the lance into his belly, but when the lance was removed, all kinds of filth and poison came out with it. Of the eleven children born to my mother, only I and five others have survived.

Out of jealousy, people tried to make my mother crawl, to humiliate her, but they never succeeded. I never saw any man, including my father, treat her disrespectfully, no matter how much they were against her. She was strong of character and inspired fear. Knowing her adversaries were too cowardly to confront her, my mother had to withstand whatever came. She was vulnerable only through her children. She did her best to protect our lives, and her vast knowledge of medicinal plants was acquired partly in her search for remedies that could help us in all our illnesses and trials.

Poison Arrows

One day when I was six years old I was going out to play. I liked to wrestle with the other boys and was successful at bringing them to the ground. I was standing in the vestibule of my home when two small arrows suddenly hit me in the chest. You can still see the scars today. They were poisoned arrows and hit me at the level of my heart. No one in the family, not even my mother, knew the antidote for the poison. The wounds became worse and I became progressively weaker but remained conscious. Elders came to see me and tried all the remedies they knew without success. They told my mother she would lose me and had to let me go. It remains in my memory as if it were yesterday: I was listening as I was almost condemned to death.

One day another elder came, Bakari Oulougueme, of the Dogon tribe. He looked at me closely and told my mother, "Someone else is going to die."

She exclaimed, "What? Someone besides Yaya?"

The elder answered, "This one is not going to die. I will save him."

I was half asleep, lying emaciated on the bed. I heard this and opened my eyes to see the old man.

He continued, "If I had come here five days later, he would have died. You would have buried him."

My mother asked him, "Will the boy be able to do anything again?"

I was in poor condition. Previously I had walked, run, won at wrestling against all the boys my age. Now I could not even lift my legs, I had to be carried. We had recently lost my little brother, and only my little sister remained unharmed.

The Dogon elder said, "I know what this is. I am going to find the guilty person and warn him. If anything else happens to one of your children, he will discover what I am capable of."

He gave me herbal remedies and played a small guitar in a lively manner. He cared for me. At the end of five days, the wound had dried out. I began to eat and walk again. Soon I was back in shape and running.

Another elder saw me. He said that for my protection I had to wear a chain around my neck that hung down my back. I grew up like that. Another elder, Mansha Kone, came to give me a protective bath. He boiled water in a calabash in front of me, added special things to it, and bathed my entire body. It burned. He said no one would ever be able to harm me again. If anyone tried to use sorcery against me, that person would die. That reassured me.

Herding and Music

After that I was a herder. As the only son in the family, I was given too much work. I had to care for a horse, go to the river for its water, cut grass for it, carry out its excrement. Because I did not even have time to wash my hands, I suffered from ascariasis, a nematode worm infestation of the intestines. I had to go looking for the donkey also. My relatives sent me out in the mornings with a herd of sheep and a herd of calves at the same time. In the evenings, I had to milk the cows. The hyenas came at night to attack the herds, and I had to be on guard and chase them away in the dark. In the morning I was back at my duties with the horse. I worked as no slave had worked. Despite all that, I was branded as lazy by my relatives, as if I had not diligently done my human best.

I had only one shirt. At the moment the rain clouds gathered, my relatives put the herds outside. The rain fell on me. I walked through the forest behind the herds, barefooted, exposed to snakes. When I became too tired, I slept wherever I was, without shelter. If I had refused these labors, I would have been beaten with sticks and verbally abused.

I could not even speak with my mother about my difficulties.

She forbade it and said, "I have lost so many children. I do not have any more tears to cry for you."

When I came to her to complain, she said, "Go, even if they kill you, go, because I do not have any more tears. Manage for yourself." My father said nothing.

I could run to my paternal grandmother's and find some protection, but I was not able to stay there long. Because she was a midwife, many women from Fienso and several surrounding villages came to her home to give birth. At the moment of labor, they put me out, with blows from sticks raining on my back.

In any free time I had, I would sit beside my mother, who cared for the disturbed people who came to her for help and who talked with the elders who came for conversation. She was a respected healer who specialized in helping the psychologically imbalanced. Her own hardships in life had only served to deepen her compassion. She had learned much about healing from her father and continually augmented this knowledge. Any severity I may have experienced from her was ultimately aimed at strengthening me and putting me on a good path.

It was difficult to find time to have fun with others during that early period when I was overtaxed with work. As much as possible, I played the drums and sang. I was also learning to play the balafon kept in my father's hut. When others went to work in the fields and I was left at home, my grandmother took down the balafon, which hung from a nail high on the wall, and I played to my heart's content. Forgetting all hardships, I immersed myself in the wonder of this music. Sometimes I played with such enthusiasm that I managed to break a calabash resonator under the balafon. In addition to playing my father's balafon, I made my own child's variation by cutting millet stalks of different lengths and arranging them on stones so that I created the appropriate scale. Practicing on this instrument helped me to commit to memory many rhythms and melodies.

When I did not have access to either my father's balafon or my own millet-stalk version, I tapped my fingers on my cheeks and made different tones by modulating the opening and closing of my mouth. Thus I assimilated the music of the balafon in a very natural way through much listening and playing in the true sense of the word. No formal course of instruction was necessary. Almost every evening the balafon was played in the village square. I could listen to and observe players of all ages. My own intrinsic drive to learn sustained my progressive mastery of the instrument in much the same way one learns to walk and talk.

Music was always present in our daily life in village celebrations, ceremonies, and as accompaniment to work and play. I was exposed to it day and night. It moved me, inspired me, filled me. During my long hours with the herds, I passed the time in contemplating the music by listening to it with my inner ears.

As a young boy, I learned to dance on a human belly. Mansha Kone, the elder who had washed me to protect me, played with me like this. He had been a close friend of my paternal grandfather, who was deceased. He treated me as he would his own child and did everything he could for me. He used to hold me over his belly so I could jump up and down on it. His stomach was like a trampoline. He made me laugh. These were happy moments. I would slip and fall, and he would tease me that I had no balance, so I learned to keep my balance.

To most of the people in the family, I seemed nonchalant and lazy. I was even considered mentally retarded. The brothers labeled me an imbecile and told me I would never succeed in life. Their wives cried out that I was worthless, good for nothing. Their jealousy did not allow them to see me as I was. Hatred was so thick in our family, you could cut it with a knife. Some said that having a child like Yaya was like having nothing at all. The other women taunted my mother, "Oh, do you think you brought a child into this world?"

I was a reject, a fool. My only error was being the eldest child in the family. That is why they gave me the impossible job of herding the calves and the sheep together. I had to walk with these poorly matched animals between the cultivated fields. All day long I would listen to the sound of the calves grazing and the birds singing. It was training in patience, in being content to be alone, and in internalizing the music that ultimately became my life's calling. I derived much pleasure from listening with my auditory memory to the balafons, drums, and other instruments.

Unexpectedly, the calves would decide to run. I ran after them, only to receive a spanking from the farmer whose field had been trampled by the calves. While this peasant was spanking me, the sheep would turn around and go onto someone else's field, where another spanking awaited me. In the evening, these people went to our compound to complain about my negligence. They insulted me, said I was worthless, cursed, a good-for-nothing fool.

One woman, recognized in the village as crazy, held the opposite view from the general opinion. She called out in a loud voice, "There are mothers with tons of children, but to have one like Yaya, that is sufficient."

My mother begged her, "Don't say that so loudly, or they will kill this one, too."

Once I was walking by the well. The supposedly foolish woman was there with other women. She cried out, "Ah, what a valuable child he is. There is no one else like him."

The others became angry. "You think that? Even in his family nobody likes him!"

Then they beat her. They said she was crazy and should not be listened to. The fact that she saw me as worthy justified them all the more in seeing her as a fool. It was as if my foolishness increased hers.

Nangape, the elder who was to become my music teacher, believed in me and saw more in me than anyone else did. He looked at me and said to my mother, "Hey, he will be a great man there. If you could know the whole journey he is going to make in his life, you would not believe it."

My mother did not dare to believe him. She maintained that we would see how I turned out once I had grown up.

3

VILLAGE LIFE

Many **Minianka proverbs** are about music. According to one, "When the music changes, the dance step must change also." This tells about music and dance of course, but it is also a message to individuals and to the community. We need to respond appropriately to the changing circumstances of life and not to become fixed.

Another proverb states, "The small drum has its voice, as does the large drum." This implies that just as no two drums are identical, no two beings are the same either. Yet each deserves to be listened to and has something to contribute to the whole. The elders may speak words of value, but so may the children. In our village councils, everyone has a right to speak about any problem that concerns him or her.

An attitude of mutual acceptance is partly a function of living close to the edge of subsistence. Disharmonies in a work group could reduce productivity and mean not enough food for the coming season. Each worker's best contribution is truly needed. This is also Minianka egalitarianism, as reflected in our proverb about the large and the small drum. Everyone is valued despite differences. This does not mean that we all get along in the village.

THOSE WHO REFUSE THE MASTER

Some people only have to get near one another to produce an atmosphere of tension. If I know a certain man with whom I cannot get along is in a work group, I will not join that group or play for it. The smallness of the village makes it possible to forestall difficulties in this way. We know one another well enough to know where we are welcome and unwelcome.

Communal life is the justification of Minianka society, and the interests of the community take precedence over those of the individual. An individual is linked to those outside the family through age groups and circles based on the work one does.

Age Groups

The age group is an important social grouping of individuals of the same sex and the same age. The organization is informal, without a designated leader, and each individual can come into full bloom. Within a group, everything in the nature of insults and tricks is permitted. Liberties are also allowed between the members of an age group and all of their children. I can be very free with the people in my father's and mother's age groups. All decisions are made by consensus among the members of an age group and remain their secret. The group must stay together through the best and the worst, in joy and in pain, and comes to the aid of any member who is in trouble.

This communal cell is very important in the development of the child because it constitutes his first contact with the world outside his family. The rules of the game are very precise. Their application is unpitying but also just, and playful childhood adventures become training for future group adhesion. When the age group decides to make some mischief or tell a lie, they are sworn to secrecy, even from their own parents. They must all do it together and submit to being hit by the same stick in punishment. In the boys' age group the sneaky, the timorous, and the traitors are cast out and chased. If a boy is given a nickname he does not like and protests, he will be subject to much joking. Another boy may be fat and find it difficult to accept this fact. He will be teased and called names to the ultimate effect that he comes to accept his condition. The watchword is justice for all by all. The ancestors watch the pre-initiation boys' age group most closely as, in the patrilineal system, the future of the village belongs to it.

VILLAGE LIFE

I remember how my age group helped me overcome my dizziness at heights. My age mates took turns climbing the palm trees to gather nuts to eat. When it was my turn, I excused myself by saying, "My grandmother told me it is very dangerous." The other boys rejoined that their grandmothers said the same thing. From that day onward, when the boys shared the nuts among themselves, they did not give any to me. Spurred on by this, I asked one of my close friends to teach me how to climb. When the others saw that I took the same risks as the rest of them, they were happy to share with me again.

The structure of girls' age groups is similar to that of the boys' circle, but unlike the boys, they will not stay with the same age group for their entire lives. The girls know they will marry when they are around sixteen or eighteen years old and move to the homes of their husbands, possibly in other villages. Each bride will become integrated into the women's group of her husband's community. At the time of a funeral in the village of origin, the women who had married into other communities will return and see one another, but no longer as members of a formal age group, just as friends who had shared their childhoods together.

One way to look at the difference between the girls' and boys' age groups is their respective roles in relation to the ancestors. The boys are the stable elements, who remain in the community to carry on the ancestral customs and lineage. Upon marrying, the girls become the potential mothers for the rebirth of their husbands' ancestors. The males stay directly responsible to their own ancestors, whereas the females become bonded to their husbands' ancestors.

Wives are emissaries for the ancestors, however, so girls must be well educated. They represent their communities of origin and their ancestors to the other communities into which they marry. The pride, self-respect, and reputation of their original communities depend on the women's upholding moral standards of behavior. In their age group, they are oriented by the adult women toward activities appropriate for mothers of families. They are prepared for their first menstruation, marriage, sexual relations within the marriage bond, pregnancy, childbirth, the responsibilities of caring for children, and the duties of being the representatives of their communities.

At the time of their initiation, which includes excision of the

Girls of Fienso.

clitoris, the girls are separated from the community for three months. During this time and throughout their upbringing, the girls are watched over by the elder women. Each girl has one grandmother, who takes special care to educate her fully and properly to become the nucleus and educator of her future family and to develop the internal strength to make personal sacrifices for the protection and well-being of her children. For example, she learns strict rules of conduct for pregnancy. She will not smoke or drink alcohol or engage in stressful transactions while a baby gestates within her. Some of her education in her age group deals with such sound, simple principles as these, which are aimed at keeping her in harmony with nature.

Every married person is considered an adult. There are several adult age groups, which serve as liaisons between the elders and the children. The adult men are initiated together into many activities, therefore they know one another's capacities and aptitudes very well. Discipline is flexible within the adult male age groups, and certain human weaknesses are pardoned. Still, free speech and practical jokes or tricks remain. After learning the customs well enough, the adults are responsible for initiation, and they play an important role in education. They are strict with the children but not abusive.

The adult women's age groups unite all the women married during the same period. These groups are oriented toward the family. Among the Minianka, the women also make up teams for working in the fields, where they are accompanied by their favorite musician. While maintaining a proper respect, I can still joke with the women of my mother's age group.

Work

In addition to belonging to their age group, people are joined together according to their work, trade, or craft. This is widespread in West Africa. The principal occupations are agriculture, fishing, hunting, cattle raising, and handicrafts. Each profession has its special music, dance steps, and dances.

The farmers make up the majority. They are not migrant but are attached to the earth, which is not always generous. They remain animists when others convert, and they have the most highly developed sense of community. They may also practice trades such as hunting, fishing, or raising goats. They are unjustly called the enemies of progress by advocates of development because they are reluctant to adopt modern technology. Instead, they respect the customs of the ancestors, which change very little.

Among the Minianka, certain people like fishing more than others and furnish the community with fresh and smoked fish. Furthermore, some villages or groups of villages organize communal fishing. The fishermen are those who know the waterways, and their beliefs always refer to water.

In each village live families of hunters, often descended from warrior families. These are often courageous people who know the bush. Their hunting and rituals are primarily done at night, and they have the reputation of being sorcerors and magicians. They dress eccentrically in earthen colored clothes and diverse hair styles, and other people fear them. Masters in the use of arms, they make their own gunpowder with a secret ritual known only to the initiated. Their dance and music are bizarre by Minianka standards, and they are the most agile and quick-moving among the people. No one else in the village dares to venture among them when they are celebrating.

The cattle herders are usually nomadic Fulani. They are at the same time the enemies and friends of the farmers. They are enemies because their animals like to eat the young sprouts or destroy the harvests. Yet they are friends because they have milk to sell or trade for agricultural produce. Moreover, the farmers like to see them with their herds on the fields as the excrement of the cattle is good fertilizer. The herders also provide animals for sacrifices during certain ceremonies and, with the coming of the plough, bulls for traction power. The Fulanis used to be the principal veterinarians, too, but some have become sedentarized and taken up agriculture.

The artists and artisans are generally called the people of the crafts. These are people who can transform natural objects into products for daily use, worship, and art. They are endowed with great knowledge. Since the beginnings of society, artisans were among those with the most sensitivity, imagination, creativity, and initiative. The group includes blacksmiths, woodworkers, shoe-makers, rope workers, potters, and musicians, all very strongly involved in the life of the village. They are also the storytellers and masters of the word.

The smiths need to be mentioned apart from the other crafts-people. They have the gift of working with metals. Previously they even extracted from the earth the minerals from which they made the tools. They are geologists, miners, and artisans. In West African society, the smith is also the sorcerer, who can manipulate powers of the invisible world. He is in contact with the entire community. Man of the night, magician, genius of rhythm, master of ceremonies of certain religious rituals, he abides as the nucleus of the traditional society. He is respected and feared by everyone except the Fulani herders. He works with water and fire, metal and wood, air and solids, the visible and the invisible. The smiths are skilled in working wood as well as metals.

The wives of the smiths are usually the potters. They make the earthenware utensils used for cooking food and the jars and jugs that conserve drinking water.

By reading about family structure, age groups, and occupational categories, you can imagine the complexity of social relations

among the Minianka. To start with, the elders want to be treated
with absolute respect, and in traditional Africa, age is indeed respected. The elders' eyes and ears are everywhere. Their language
is rich in parables and seems obscure to the young. They often
have recourse to proverbs: The elders are the subject of the next
chapter.

4

THE ELDERS

Grandparents form the circle of the elders. They represent the world of knowledge and constitute the supreme council of the village. To avoid the anger of the ancestors, with whom they can communicate through rituals and divination, they are supposed to know all the prohibitions and how to remedy any violation of a social taboo. They are wise and move thoughtfully. They are walking books of know-how. They are the judges, lawyers, catalysts, negotiators, moderators, moralizers, critics, and counselors.

In a Minianka village, if an elder passes along the road with baggage, he is surrounded by children to relieve him of his load. This is done instinctively and requires no payment. It is necessary to greet elders when one comes across them. When one asks them questions, they always say they do not know or give evasive answers. They take time to judge whether or not the questioner deserves an answer. They can listen to a liar and afterwards exclaim the person's name: "Hey, Diallo," or "Hey, Kone. The man who says he is married to an invisible wife sleeps alone at night." This means you may fool others, but not yourself.

It is in the best interests of youth to please the elders since, during certain initiations, the latter can be unpitying. Further-more, if it happened that one really needed them, they would take account of one's prior conduct.

Unfortunately, they are becoming distrustful and less easily ap-proachable. They lack confidence that the youth have gone through the appropriate initiations and partake of traditional val-ues. The young people no longer look up to the elders as role models.

In my youth, I aspired only to become like Nangape, the elder who taught me music. Now, the village elders no longer represent what the young hope to achieve, and the elders themselves do not want to waste their time talking with youth who are not listening, who lack discernment and clear reasoning.

Having traveled, the younger generation thinks they know more than the elders, who have always lived in the village. The elders are pejoratively referred to as "fish in a well." Evidently, such fish are limited in their knowledge of the waters of the world and can never reach the vastness of the ocean.

Nowadays, when the youth approach the elders, it is to seek help with problems. For example, a young man wants a young woman to be attracted to him alone, or he wants to know how to get a particular job. The elders are not interested in this.

The elders are attached to customs and want to preserve them. They take care of community harmony. They preside over the village council under the tree of dialogue. Everyone has the right to speak there, but to be advanced in age and to be reasonable are two different things; no one overlooks that. What the majority decide is held to be the truth, even if the majority are wrong.

In the children's age groups they learn that the individual by himself possesses nothing. The children are the hope of the com-munity. A proverb states, "The young sprout permits one to pre-dict the height of the tree." From the conduct of the young, one foresees the future of the community. The elders teach the chil-dren games, and it is expected that they will follow the rules without the supervision of a referee.

When I was a child, the elders often tested me and the other youth to see if we were worthy of receiving transmissions of knowl-edge. We never knew when we were being tested; this way the elders could see if we were attentive, observant, capable of follow-ing directions. When we passed our tests, we were entrusted with secrets. A few stories from my own experience illustrate the kinds of tests the elders gave us.

Once I was passing some elders who were seated in the shade of a great baobab tree in the village square. Calling me over, they instructed me to gather certain herbs. After that, I was to find three special stones and arrange them in a designated way on the ground just at the entry gate of my family compound. Then I was to take a clay pot, put some water, the stones, and the herbs into it, cover the pot with its lid, mix ashes with a little water, and put the ashes between the pot and cover around the rim. Finally, I was to heat up the entire mixture.

I did everything I was told with one exception that did not seem to make any difference to me. Instead of putting ashes around the rim of the pot, I put wet clay. Having seen my mother do this often as she made medicinal brews, I thought it would be an acceptable way to seal the pot. How wrong I was!

Back at the village square, the elders asked me to recount exactly what I had done. I confidently did so. However, as soon as I mentioned the clay I had put between the pot and cover, I was ordered to go back and do my task again.

An elder commented, "He is not ready yet."

When I asked my mother why the elders were so angry with me, she answered, "Ashes have medicinal properties also. When the water boils, some of the ash falls into the mixture. Clay has its properties as well. There is no standard method. Each mixture must be prepared exactly as directed. If not, some vital balance could be disturbed to the detriment of a person who imbibes the brew."

In the West, a pharmacist or doctor who forgets a formula can look it up and read it in the appropriate reference manual. For villagers whose entire heritage has been transmitted by word of mouth, this is not possible. An exacting following of directions from memory is essential.

On another occasion, an elder sent me to get a special tobacco. Assuming it made no difference who went for the tobacco, I sent a younger brother of mine for it. Just as it was my duty to follow the elder, it was my little brother's duty to follow me. Only one old woman in the village grew this sort of tobacco. She told my brother she had no more of it and sent him back to me empty-handed.

The elder became very angry with me for not having gone personally to the woman. In fact, I had to go after all. To my surprise, when I asked for the tobacco, I received it. As it turned out, there was a conflict between the man and the woman that I had not known about. She would have refused the tobacco to anyone else in the village except me because of a special relationship between her and me. The elder who asked for the tobacco had correctly determined that I was the only one who could perform the task. Furthermore, he was looking to see if I was willing to make personal sacrifices of my own time for him. This was not an arbitrary exercise of his authority over me. To the contrary, in our culture, making oneself available for the needs of the people is accorded a very high value. A musician, for example, might be called on at any hour of the day or night to perform at an important ceremony. Technical versatility on the drum, while appreciated, is not considered as crucial as the musician's good will and readiness to serve.

The same issue about my being available came up differently in another incident when I was about ten years old. An elder sent me on an errand to his wife. He said, "Go tell my wife to look for the money I left in a pocket in my clothes at home. She is to give it to my son who should buy some meat with it."

When I saw that his son was not in, I went back to the old man with this news. I lengthened my road with this round trip for nothing. He said to me, "If my son is not at home, could you not be my son and do the favor for me?"

This elder was not content just to yell at me for not helping him. He came to my family and said I did not want to assist the elders. He cited the proverb, "If you send the chicken to market to buy some meat, it is in the interest of the chicken to come back with some meat." I was the chicken, and the elders judged me not ready for some knowledge they might have imparted to me.

In the incidents involving the ashes and the tobacco, I was faulted by elders for not doing exactly what I had been asked. In the case of the meat, my error was not realizing that I too could be considered the old man's son. In each case, I failed to extend myself as much as possible for the sake of others in my community. That was the most important lesson I needed to learn.

Nangape

Nangape Kone, my music teacher and defender in the village, was the elder who gave me my greatest lessons.

THOSE WHO REFUSE THE MASTER

When I was a boy, Nangape, with his white beard and inner authority, seemed very old to me, even though he was not even as old as my grandfather. As a five-year-old, I saw him as an elder of the greatest age. Even now that I have grown up, I have not been able to change my image of him and imagine him still towering over me in height. The last time I saw Nangape was in 1965, when I was nineteen years old. We spoke, and he gave me much advice. Then he informed me that perhaps we would never see each other again. In 1967, when I returned to the village after completing high school, Nangape was gone. At that time, I was full of pride over having passed the baccalaureate examination and being given the opportunity to continue my studies at the college level overseas. While I spent my three months of vacation in the village, I did not even once go to greet Nangape's widow. It is painful for me to remember this. His widow had been the mother of my apprenticeship in music and traditional culture. Nangape had been my defender, my lawyer, my psychotherapist. When she was dying, Nangape's widow confided in my mother that she could not understand my withdrawal and silence toward her. This woman had been very kind to me from an early age. As a youngster, I went so many nights to Nangape's to listen to his music. Often I fell asleep by his balafon. When I awoke, I found myself at my grandmother's and was temporarily disoriented, as I remembered falling asleep at Nangape's. His wife had carried me each time to my grandmother's so I could sleep comfortably. She also spoke up in my defense whenever the older women saw fault in my character. When I finally realized how I had neglected to speak with Nangape's widow and to acknowledge all they had meant to me, I arranged to make amends for this through the proper rituals.

In the village of Fienso, Nangape was the guardian of the *n'peen-yee* drums and the balafons that went with them. They were housed in the back of the first hut inside the gateway to Nangape's compound.

The n'peenyee is a long drum made of a hollowed-out tree trunk with goatskin on each end. The musician sits on it with one leg to each side. This drum is played in sets of three of the same shape but different sizes by three drummers. These drums are the father, the mother, and the child. The players of the first two also have a bell. The drummers strike the drum heads with a stick to make one rhythm and create a different rhythm with the bells. The smallest drum gives the basic tone. The effect of the combined drum and bell rhythms is to resonate with different parts of the listeners' bodies: the drums affect the torso, and the bells the head. Two balafons always accompany this music and add to its rhythmic complexity.

The n'peenyee music is played for all occasions that touch on the invisible realms, such as burials, funerals, the sacred wood ceremony, and the annual festival for the Creator, Kle. Apprentice musicians are present to observe and feel the effects of the music as part of their preparation for the time they will play.

I have played the balafon and the smallest drum in these ensembles but never the father or the mother drums. Nangape played all these instruments, sang, and gave incantations before playing to ensure the protection of all the musicians.

Nangape was the simplest man I ever saw. He stood about five-feet-eight inches tall and was thin, with strong, well-defined muscles. Usually he was bare-chested, with only a loincloth on his torso. I never saw him wear shoes. His small white beard highlighted the bottom line of his chin. A plain white cotton cap that showed the dust of our land covered the top of his head. I saw no luxuries at his home, which was a simple, round, mud hut with a thin grass mat on the floor for sleeping. He married one wife and lived devoted to her. They had one son. Nangape cultivated one field and grew just enough food to feed his family. He was well liked and respected, a master musician, a seer. He participated in all the village ceremonies. At those times, he wore a long robe. When he went to other villages to play, he would also wear cotton trousers, sewn in our local style with wide, loose legs. In his daily life in the village, he had no need for such clothes. Everything about him was so simple that it touched on poverty. One wondered how he could be so poor in material things, yet so dignified. However, money and his lifestyle were irreconcilable. He possessed virtually nothing and envied no one. He was devoted to his calling, music. One of his roles in training the younger musicians was to kill our egos. He was exemplary, egoless.

I told Nangape's son how much his father had helped me. He was moved and said, "Yes, he was your elder, after all. Everyone knows that."

I told the son that I realized his father's greatness suddenly one day. I had traveled, met all sorts of people, millionaires, great speakers. He preferred to stay quietly at home and not to visit other people's houses. In all the time I grew up in the village, I never saw him go to anyone else's home for a social visit. If he came to another family's compound, it was not a good thing because it meant he was going to play N'Peenyee for a funeral. In normal circumstances, if he needed to give a message to anyone else in the village, he would send a youth.

Nangape did not speak much. He was silent most of the time, but if he said something would happen, you would be sure to see it occur. For this reason, Nangape never made a bad wish. He was serious. If he told you something about yourself, he was so accurate that it seemed he had read your destiny.

Nangape had the inner strength to abstain from whatever was superfluous in life. When I speak of him, people think I am referring to another century and forget I am a contemporary man. Nangape was a man of this century also. His goal was to train the young people of the village. He never took advantage of us. Unlike some other elders, he did not make us work like slaves at his home. We came to greet him, to offer our services, and he would ask for a little help only. If he asked me to run an errand or do a chore for him, I was glad to help. Sometimes I refused, though, and he accepted this because he knew I was overworked with the family herds and studies for school. He also knew my future was not to be involved with the labors of the village but with other challenges.

When my paternal grandmother fell ill, I was the intermediary who asked Nangape to treat her. He was the one person in the village who knew best how to care for her. Every time she needed remedies, he sent me to look for them. Nangape knew I loved my grandmother. He taught me how to give my grandmother the herbs. I placed them over coals, she leaned over the herbs and breathed the aromatic vapors. This brought her relief. Working together to help my grandmother, Nangape and I reinforced the ties between us.

I used to fear that Nangape's family would disappear, since he had only one son. However, this son has had many children, so the family line will continue. Unfortunately, the n'peenyee orchestra is going to disappear. Although the orchestra is still there, the musicians do not get along well; they lack a true leader. The son learned things from his father, but I do not have the same closeness with the son that allows me to ask him questions. The father shared knowledge freely with me; the son keeps his paternal heritage more to himself. Still, whenever I go to Fienso, I go the son's compound to greet him. I am moved when I see the hut where Nangape slept.

When other musicians of the village see me, they call out, "Oh, there goes the friend of our great teacher." The relation between me and most of them stops there. One exception is N'Yago. He is a true friend of mine and another of Nangape's favorite students. He learned a lot about plants from our old master and is generous in sharing his knowledge with me. He is altruistic, as opposed to many of Nangape's former students, who use whatever they learned from the father to compete with the son.

The cause of the competition is the introduction of the profit motive. Traditional healing work is becoming more lucrative: fees are set for specific treatments, a thing unheard of and impossible in my youth. It hurt me to see that the desire for money has corrupted many musicians. Each one is a healer in his own corner. They have lost something of the true sense of community.

KNOWLEDGE

Among the Minianka, the world is divided into two realms: the visible and the invisible. The invisible world borders the visible and contains all that we do not see, such as spirits and ancestors. No one can say where one realm ends and the other begins, either in time or in space. The human being exists in both realms. When we look at one another, we see forms of flesh, more or less agreeable to behold. These are our visible aspects only, not our true selves. Our visible forms maintain us, but our real being is invisible and interior.

Kle is the Supreme Being, God, the creator of all. This word is always singular, never plural. Kle was not and cannot be created but gave rise to everything else. Kle is undefined, infinite, unknowable, the master of both the visible and the invisible. To enter into contact with Kle, one goes by way of an intermediary such as a stream. Outsiders may mistakenly think the Minianka worship the stream itself. The Minianka never directly summon Kle; they always use an intermediary such as a stone, a fetish, or the ancestors, who are already in the invisible realm.

A fetish is a ritual object, such as a mask or a statue, that is endowed with occult power. A secret mixture made of animal blood and several plants is placed on a mask or statue to make a fetish. The fetish is not a god, and it is not worshipped by the people: it is a means of bringing together a group of people around a certain aspect of knowledge. The particular formulas used are known only to the initiates of secret societies responsible for the fetish. Possibly no one today can say why specific ingredients go into a fetish. The ancestors found certain mixtures to be efficacious and potent, and for contemporary practitioners of the traditional rituals that is enough reason to use them. Foreigners have sometimes claimed that the Minianka are polytheists who worship divinities of the forest and of the water. These outsiders have not understood the practice of going through intermediaries to the one divinity, who is omnipresent and can hear the people. Whereas Kle does not need the intermediaries to hear the people, humans need the intermediaries to summon Kle. This shows appropriate reverence for the divine.

The huts in the village are traditionally round, except for one square hut in the middle of the village: this is *Kle-goa,* the house of Kle. Its walls and roof are made of earth, and it is oriented to the four cardinal directions. Each of the walls has a door, but one must not enter this hut, which stands expressly for community prayers, for any purpose other than the sanctioned rituals for which it was built. The Minianka will not live in a village unless such a hut is maintained there and either repaired or rebuilt each year.

Inside Kle-goa is a stone that symbolizes humility for the Minianka and over which sacrifices are made at an annual ceremony. At the ceremony, the traditional chiefs and high initiates pray together for the well-being of the entire community. Music is played, and a rooster is sacrificed as an offering from the community to the invisible world.

To keep peace and balance in the cosmos, there is an entire system of rules known as *Kle-kolo,* the path that Kle has laid out. These rules are necessary for peace in the family, the community, nature, the wider universe, and the invisible world. The whole community organization teaches Kle-kolo. Every "do this" and "don't do that," every reprimand and slap teaches it. The ancestors in the invisible world help to ensure that the rules are being followed.

THOSE WHO REFUSE THE MASTER

One does not abstain from certain actions out of fear of the police or of prison, but because one should not do them along the path of God and because of potential negative consequences from the invisible world. Forbidden actions performed in hiding are visible to the ancestors, who will punish the offender. Violating the divine rules will have negative repercussions on the family, the community, nature, and the cosmos. These rules constitute a sort of ecology of the visible and invisible worlds. They concern not only human relations but also relations with plants, between plants and animals, and so on.

The whole of knowledge available in the cosmos is called *n'kie.** It includes the experience of the ancestors, who have left customs, traditions, and philosophy as a legacy. A person can also acquire certain powers and knowledge through the intermediary of the double, that invisible part of a human being. While the term *sorcerer* refers to an individual who has acquired knowledge and power, including the power to affect people at a distance through spirits, a distinction must be made according to whether the sorcerer uses the knowledge wisely or harmfully. The difference between an evil sorcerer and a good one is the color of the interior, which is explained later. A person with a red interior might acquire knowledge and power, alas, just as well as a person with a white interior.

Another sort of knowing is that practiced by the seer, *wogne n'kiefolo,* who can predict the future and whose vision of reality cannot be explained. The seer is not necessarily a sorcerer. The seer has the power of vision but not necessarily the power to affect other people through spirits.

The sum of acquired knowledge that permits healing is known as *weree.* When it is said of a person, "Wa weree n'kie," this means that he or she knows many medicinal herbs, fetishes and magical and sacred words.

My mother is respected for this kind of knowledge, and for her healing with plants and words. This knowledge is gained either from human sources, as through family secrets, or from the invisible world. My mother learned much in her family of origin, since her father was a healer. The illnesses, accidents, and hardships

---

*For music that celebrates the Minianka conception of knowledge, listen to "Kewara" on *The Healing Drum* audiocassette (see page 213 for ordering information).

experienced by her eleven children motivated her all the more strongly to seek out healing plants and formulas. Her practical work as a healer of the mentally disturbed constantly drew on her knowledge and challenged her to expand it. To this day, I don't know how far my mother's knowledge extends. She has shared some of it with me, but I know that it exceeds what I have been entrusted with.

When the term *weree* is used in the sense of a fetish, this implies above all a remedy for the society. Weree's primary role is to protect against dangers on earth. For example, the warrior's secret society, the Maniah, is in charge of a fetish built by the ancestors to protect against conquest and enslavement and to promote victory in war. The fetish of the women's secret society functions to protect against sterility, miscarriages, and mishaps in childbirth. Because the knowledge about how to use the fetishes is kept secret, little can be written about them. In the following chapter we look at how the secret society functions in terms of the society as a whole.

The Human Being

Tipia is the word that means human being. Like the English words *human, humane,* and *humanity,* Tipia also connotes kindness. The human being is thought by the Minianka to be composed of four interrelated parts. The first of these is the visible part, the body, called *n'kere.* The second part is *minan,* the vital principle, the breath that animates the body, life itself. Literally, it means nose. Thanks to minan, humans can move and work; without it, we cannot participate in this world.

The third constituent of the human being is *dya.* Literally, this means the shadow; figuratively, it signifies the double—an invisible replica of the human being, imprinted with good and bad moral qualities. It belongs to the invisible realm and learns directly from that realm. It is a very mobile aspect of our nature and can even leave the body temporarily. When we are frightened and stand transfixed, it is because the double has fled the body. Until it returns, we remain immobilized. If it leaves permanently, the resulting condition is insanity. When the mentally disturbed become momentarily lucid and normal, it is because the double has returned to the body. The physical body dies when the double leaves with the last breath, that is, dya leaves with minan. *Soul* is the Western word for this combination of the double with minan. It survives death.

A sudden noise or music itself often affects the double. At night, the double may leave and travel in invisible realms, resulting in dreams or nightmares. Sometimes the double can be extraordinarily powerful and increase one's normal capacity, for example, when an unusually heavy encumbrance is lifted in an emergency that could not be lifted normally or when one momentarily leaps to safety.

One night, when I was a young boy, I experienced being empowered by my double. An uncle and I were taken by surprise by a wild beast that threatened us. It was a dangerous flesh-eater that we call *nanyaraga* in our language, but I do not know its name in English. We ran with a speed we would not have previously imagined possible to a tree thick with thorns and rapidly mounted to the top. In the morning, the danger past, we were not able to descend unaided. Our doubles gave us this life-saving nimbleness in the night.

The fourth part of the human being is called *n'fougon*, the interior. This is the center of intelligence and perception. The human interior is formed of contradictory tendencies, weaknesses and strengths. Among the weaknesses are envy, jealousy, the desire for riches and power. Among the strengths are humbleness, self-restraint, and silence. The human being needs to attain balance between the strengths and weaknesses in order to be a harmonious individual. If the weaknesses dominate, perception will be distorted through greed, lust, or whatever vice is activated. If the person becomes one-sidedly virtuous, he or she risks falling into simple-minded naiveté. One needs to integrate the strengths with the weaknesses in order to become harmonious with oneself, the community, and the cosmos.

The Minianka word for the human interior can be accompanied by specific adjectives that refer to colors to signify the disposition of the inner being. The colors are not visible in a literal sense; the words are used figuratively to indicate moral characteristics. If it is said that the interior is red, weaknesses dominate, and the person is nasty, bitter, lacking in love and self-love, capable of evil acts that harm self and others. People whose interior is red are feared.

KNOWLEDGE

The person with the white interior has achieved balance between strengths and weaknesses. These people know how to share with others. They are not envious, they feel contented with their lot in life. They consider the consequences of their actions, not only to themselves but also to their families, the community, the environment. Such people are wise, and it is the greatest of compliments to say a person's interior is white.

Black is the third condition of the human interior. This indicates a person lost in forgetfulness. The Minianka do not have a word for *forget,* they say instead that a person's interior is black. This can be temporary or a long-term state.

A dark interior indicates a condition of being closed in upon oneself. Such people are not good for others. One man in this category married three times within five years, and each of his wives died not long after the marriage. Someone with a dark interior will undermine a business venture or any group endeavor. Often such people have a way of getting the most important tasks assigned to them, and they bring on failure. They are not bad people, but they are not conscious of their actions.

The Minianka are reluctant to share all they know with others; what if the person to whom they revealed themselves had a red interior? He or she could take the information and misuse it to harm the person who had opened up unwisely. Even if the confidante were not of a red interior the information could be passed on to someone of evil disposition. The exposed person would again be at risk of sorcery or betrayal.

The Miniankan learns to perceive the color of the human interior through observing an individual's behavior in society. Someone who is characteristically dishonest and untrustworthy reveals a dark interior. Some specially gifted people are able to see beneath the surface more directly into the interior character of another, even if the person's behavior is deceptive.

The traditional Minianka education and initiations are aimed at strengthening and ensuring a good direction to the interior aspect of the human being. The youth are encouraged to attain balance, adapt to the environment, become aware and sensitive. A white interior brings benefits to the community and attracts good spirits. A red interior disturbs the community, upsets balance in the environment, and attracts evil spirits. A black interior is confused and brings confusion to the community.

THOSE WHO REFUSE THE MASTER

Diomon and Fiaga

For the Minianka, silence, *fiaga,* is the principal condition of the inner life. Fiaga is the mother of the word, or *diomon.* The word is only external; like music, it is sound, noise. The word is first of all a means of communication, but it is a double-edged sword. It can be destructive, as in the case of insults or disagreeable comments. Ceremonies attend the use of magical words, whether to bless or to curse. A word can make someone sick. Yet there are also healing words, and they are important in traditional Minianka medical practice. Headaches may be removed and calm restored through the word. Therefore, the word must be directed with intelligence. According to a Minianka proverb, "Unlike the lion, man does not have a tail by which he can be caught. Rather, catch him by his word. The word is the tail of man."

To keep silent is to cultivate one's interior dimension. The Minianka learn how to sit quietly. Many sayings reflect various aspects of silence: "Silence hides a person's way of being, the word discloses it"; "Silence is reflective, the word thoughtless"; "Silence has delimited the paths, the word has jumbled them"; "Silence has given birth to seriousness, the word to diversion"; "The secret belongs to the one who knows how to keep silent."

The Minianka affirm the value of being silent and do not feel an obligation to say everything or to make conversation needlessly. It is disconcerting to be in the company of Westerners who do not know how to appreciate being quietly in someone else's presence. It was a shock to me when I first came to Canada to find that whenever I simply wished to rest quietly within myself, I was hounded with questions. Questions like "Hey, what are you thinking about?" interrupt moments of profound self-recollection. "Is something the matter?" may be a question that rudely misconstrues an unproblematical dwelling within one's inner being.

A person who talks too much in Minianka society is not taken seriously and may not even be listened to after a while. In fact, this habit of externalizing too much in words can unbalance a person and bring on sickness. But words can reveal a confused state of mind that might be hidden in silence. The proper balance between well-chosen words and silence is an important factor in an individual's health.

KNOWLEDGE

Death

Hoou, the next concept to consider, means death. It is not regarded as the enemy of life because everything is cyclical. Death is the passage from the visible to the invisible state. While the body is no longer there, the double and the vital principle of breath continue in the invisible realm. To die is to become a human seed that could sprout again. Nonetheless, it is necessary for the living to cry for those who have died. The tears constitute the waters that are necessary for the germination of the seed. To die without being given a funeral is a sacrilege. For the old, to die well means to be buried with a great funeral.

The ancestors, those who have died, are called *houyees.* Sometimes they can enter into communication with the living through the mouth of a person whose double has departed. Sometimes they can communicate through dreams or nightmares. They caution and advise, they mediate between the visible and invisible realms, they intervene in the lives of their descendants to punish or reward. At death, they can accept or refuse the soul of the deceased. In the latter case, the dead one becomes a wandering soul.

In the Minianka cosmos, there is no hell or heaven. A person's goal is to live in such a way that he or she becomes an ancestor with the role of mediating between the visible and invisible realms, of working for harmony while enjoying proximity with the Creator. The houyees are the seeds of future incarnations into the visible world, a reserve of seeds for sowing future generations. When my son, Telli, came to Fienso for the first time, the elders recognized my maternal grandfather, who had returned as this boy. The community of ancestors decide it is time for a given soul to be born to the visible world for another turn, with specified tasks such as marriage to a certain mate. Striking similarities of temperament and other charateristics between a young person and an ancestor are taken by the Minianka to indicate not hereditary resemblance but reincarnation.

With respect to the ancestors, there is a daily form of worship. Each time one eats, a portion is set aside to offer to them. When one drinks, one pours also for the ancestors. If one happens to forget these rituals, the dishes should not be washed immediately but left for the following day. These are symbolic gestures. The material aspects of the food will not be eaten, but the vital principle in the food, an invisible aspect, will meet the ancestors in the invisible realm. Even when the living eat, the nourishment received from the food is from both its material elements and its spirit.

Spirits

The ancestors are not the only invisible neighbors of the living villagers. There are also the spirits known as *sigue-chim*, the inhabitants of the bush who live in the water and in the forest. Some people claim to see them and to enter into communication with them. Other people, such as sorcerers, are reputed to have the power of sending specific spirits against people. One must be wary of people with this power: the spirits can mount a person's double and lead it away just as one would mount and ride a horse.

The spirits can also form bonds of friendship with people. The language spoken by the spirits is not the same as human language, but certain individuals can speak it. When this occurs, it is said that these individuals have left for another world. Young children and very old people are considered close to this other world. A newborn baby's babbling is taken to be communication in spirit language, as is the speech of the elderly who have lost their reasoning and fallen into a childlike state. It is maintained that the ancestors and spirits like to play with very small children. When the children acquire the power of human speech, the invisible playmates depart, otherwise the children could explain what they are experiencing from the invisible realm.

Whenever there is dancing, the spirits come to dance also. When they take certain people as dance partners, it is called the trance state. In trances, with the help of spirits, villagers may predict misfortunes such as epidemics, floods, deaths. They may also foresee good news such as abundant harvests and healthy births. No one can say when or through which people such messages will be delivered.

Not all spirits are benefactors. Some can haunt people and disorient them, leading to the destruction of the community. These evil spirits can only operate through people whose interiors are red and people known as *sicanfolo*, sorcerers whose intentions are harmful. (Those who use noxious substances to poison people are also called *sicanfolo*.)

Evil water spirits can provoke drownings. Therefore, before going fishing, the people seek to make peace with the water spirits, sometimes by the sacrifice of a chicken. This ritual signals the water spirits that people are coming into the water and will upset them a bit. It tells the spirits to accept the fishermen.

Before cutting down a tree, one must address the tree spirits, for evil spirits can dwell in trees also. I know of a family in which nearly every member became mentally disturbed because they did not take proper precautions with the tree spirits. A tamarind tree next to their home had spirits living in it that were not very evil, but not particularly good either. When the father of the family died, the children decided to fell the tree. Two of the children immediately became disturbed and irrational.

Having lost their tree dwelling and not wanting to live alone, the spirits took up residence in the children of the family. Their speech was incomprehensible, and they cried out inexplicably. It was very difficult to rid the children of these spirits.

Another childhood friend of mine married a woman with whom he had five children. When they cut down a tree, his wife went crazy. The entire village recognized the felling of the tree as the immediate antecedent of the derangement.

Some animals become haunted by spirits, and some spirits transform themselves into animals to provoke the hunters. If the hunters shoot at these animals, they themselves die or lose their reasoning. Other spirits take on the appearance of pretty female strangers who say they are lost, get people involved with them, and kill. It is believed that spirits can enter into people, eat their doubles, and go on to destroy others. Spirits in the air, the trees, the stones, the earth, and the water surround the living and affect them.

The Minianka are not the only African people who conceive the world in this way. The Ibo and Yoruba people of Nigeria, like the Minianka, often see physical and mental illness as the result of contact with evil spirits who may have been provoked by some violation of the visible or invisible order. A healer acts, in part, as an intermediary between worlds to determine which spirits are at work and how to bring the ill person back into harmony with them. For the traditional animist, one cannot speak of mental health without taking the invisible world into account.

THOSE WHO REFUSE THE MASTER

The goal of life is to be able to fulfill a good life and then to occupy a peaceful place in the parallel community of ancestors. This implies that all people guilty of evil actions are rejected by that community and become lost and wandering souls. Africans often speak of encountering these wandering souls. Most people among the Miniaka and many other tribes wear talismans to protect themselves against ghosts and evil spirits.

For the animist, we humans are neither the center of the universe nor the only ones in control, but we must take account of our impact. This is true for all our actions, even the playing of music. When the balafon is accompanied by the flute, for example, all reptiles, including snakes, are attracted to the village. Whether one likes it or not, shoes must be worn on these occasions for protection. The musicians are responsible for playing very well since good music will calm the serpents, and bad music will irritate them. This example shows that what we do has repercussions beyond ourselves. All things are connected, and the rules that protect the integrity and viability of the whole and its parts must be preserved. Anyone who violates the rules that secure harmony among humans, spirits, ancestors, animals, and plants risks becoming psychologically disturbed.

Geomancy

Geomancy is one of the practices whereby the Minianka seek a proper relationship with the earth. Human habitations cannot be built just anywhere—the earth's own senses and spirits must be taken into account. A person who builds a house along a road at the point where another road ends is exposed to evil spirits and to the bad vibrations of the earth, according to Minianka geomancy. This is held to be very important. Similarly, the farmer does not choose the place for his fields at random. In addition to studying whether the soil is fertile or infertile, he must be careful of certain locations.

In building a house, once a site is chosen, the orientation of the walls and placing of the doors must be decided wisely. According to Minianka belief, doors facing the different points of the compass will affect the inhabitants of the dwelling differently. The public gate of a Minianka compound is oriented to facilitate the frequent passing of people. The gate of the ancestors always faces east. Its placement in relation to all the huts that comprise the compound establishes a configuration of energies through which it is safe to walk only on consecrated occasions. The public gate poses no such problems.

There are some zones between two villages where it is considered grave if two people cross paths. If two individuals find themselves heading toward such a taboo encounter, either one or the other will stop to avoid potential ill effects to both of them. In Fienso, some trees have grown in places where one must not seek shade at just any moment. Near the village is one stand of trees where it is forbidden to call anyone at noon.

According to Minianka geomancy, all spirits can meet at crossroads. Bad vibrations coincide there also, which is the reason eggs are broken sacrifically at crossroads. Seven roads enter Fienso. This is held to be auspicious and to augur prosperity for the inhabitants. At the same time, the crossing of these seven roads means that many spirits are in the village, which gives it special characteristics. As I said before, the ambiance in my village is so strongly marked by the invisible world that people wonder why its inhabitants remain. The bad spirits are, however, counterbalanced by the good ones. A kind of bargaining occurs between the two sorts, and life goes on.

INITIATIONS AND
SECRET SOCIETIES

When I was young, I was told to prepare myself to die during the circumcision. The older boys who were already circumcised told me stories. "They are going to kill you then. The spirits will come to eat your body. Your bones will be put in the middle of a crossroads. A horseman with a whip will hit the bones. You will bounce back to life and run. If he misses you, you will remain dead." Hearing such stories, I thought I might prefer not to be circumcised.

Circumcision is the first important initiation for a boy in Minianka society. Like all Senufo, we have the most initiations of any ethnic group in Africa. Circumcision occurs between the ages of ten and fourteen. Preparation goes on throughout childhood for this important rite of passage. No one tells the boys anything about the mysteries that surround the operation or what they will be taught then. Initiations were created in our culture expressly to help people realize new strengths within themselves by surmounting difficulties and voluntarily enduring suffering. Initiations are designed to enlarge the initiate's vision of the world. In Minianka, the word *initiation* itself implies "to die." Through the trials of the initiation, old routines are broken, and the initiate moves on to the next stage. We say, "They killed me in the initiation ceremony," or even "They killed me in the marriage ceremony." Marriage is understood in our culture as an initiation. The bride or groom loses individual liberty to become bonded to another person. Concessions will have to be made by each partner in consideration of the other. Old habits must die for new ones to be established.

Circumcision

Once a year in the village square we saw the dance of those who had been circumcised six months earlier. They were just returning to the village after a retreat in the forest. Their dance looked really good. We boys had never seen them do anything like it before. We thought, "Maybe on our return from the circumcision, we could dance and play like that, too."

On the eve of the operation, when our turn had come, the drums were played, and there was dancing in the village. The particular rhythms and the dance of the former initiates and the elders indicated that the following day there would be a circumcision of all the boys of our age group. We watched the music and dancing but could not participate.

At four in the morning, we were each awakened from our sleep by a paternal uncle. There was a serious tone, not the usual playfulness. "Get your clothes and dress fast." "What is happening?" we asked. "No questions," we heard in response. Walking outside, we saw other boys gradually assembling in the village. One by one, we were taken into the forest in order of age, the oldest first. We heard nothing, and the boys didn't return. It was hard. We had all been told countless times throughout childhood not to cry or scream, no matter what pain we felt. To do so would dishonor our families. I was the last to be taken. I didn't know what to expect. If only I had been in the middle, it would have been over already. I felt almost dead from fright.

After the operation, we stayed in the bush with the elders. It was time for discipline to start. "Your grandmothers are no longer to wash you," they told us. "You are capable of feeding yourselves and doing everything for yourselves—don't depend on anyone else for that any more. No more children's games. Your childhood is over. You had fun. It is time to stop childish pranks. You understand a lot now."

During the six months spent in the woods with the elders, we had no grandmothers, mothers, or fathers to comfort us. The mothers brought meals out to the woods, but we weren't permitted to communicate with them.

The initiates make and use a special musical instrument during the initiation camp. It consists of a stick, with calabashes at one end, that is shaken back and forth to make a rattling sound. The boys are taught to play special rhythms with it and to sing certain songs. When they return to the village, as happens periodically during the retreat, they play this instrument. On the day they will return to their homes, they break it at the crossroads.

During this six-month period, when the initiates return to the village periodically their purpose is either to act as moral educators or to steal. They ask an elder for money, then leave it in the open, and hide themselves where they can watch the money. They wait for the adults, their teachers of morality, to pass by. There is irony in the situation: the adult sees the money, then he looks all around to see if anyone else is observing. If he feels safe, he bends down to pick up the money. At this moment, the initiates leap out of hiding, shake their calabash rattles, and cry out, "Thief!" To save his reputation, the adult gives the boys even more money and asks them not to tell anyone else. If the adult tries to run with the money, the boys pursue him to his home, singing, playing the music, and dancing. They cannot dance too much yet, though, because their wounds are still healing. As village educators, they relish this turning of the tables on those who not long before were spanking them.

Curiously, before returning to the bush, they are allowed the privilege of stealing a chicken for the dinner sauce that evening. No one protests.

During the initiation retreat, the boys get intensive training in music and dance. They will not perform these rhythms again unless they are given the responsibility of being initiators when they themselves are elders. The retreat teaches them other things as well: they learn to work in community, and they develop discipline among themselves. The elders teach them which wild plants to use for varied purposes and which to avoid. This is an obligatory initiation.

INITIATIONS AND SECRET SOCIETIES

Fire Initiation

The next initiation for Minianka males is the test of fire. The ceremonies for this initiation occur once every seven years. It opens the door for other initiations.

It frustrates me very much that because of my schooling and the timing of the ceremonies I was never able to go through the test of fire. The music of these initiates is the most wonderful. When I am in the village, and they play it at night, I cannot participate and have to go to bed since I am not initiated. The goal of the initiation is to learn to subdue fire.

A Malian living in Montreal who had passed this initiation was able to save the people in a burning apartment building. He had no fear of fire. He also knows of plants to put on his body to protect against burns and to heal them, but he does not make use of this knowledge in Montreal.

Some initiates of this test of fire are burned. It is a very serious initiation. At the death of an elder, the fire initiates do a complicated dance that no one else can do. It requires long training and is incredible to see: they jump into the fire. Their clothes burn, but the flames do not hurt them. Their dance is acrobatic, their music excellent. They are able to enjoy themselves with fire. This initiation is obligatory for men who live in the village, as is the preparation for marriage.

The initiations of which we have spoken so far are all required of the village men. After these, the men can chose to be initiated into the secret societies.

The goal of the secret societies is to learn to master forces of the visible and invisible realms for the benefit of the community. They also intercede with the ancestors on behalf of the living, although they are not directly concerned with human relations with the divine. There are some people who are inclined to misuse the powers they have gained for evil ends, but the secret societies exercise control to ensure that their initiates serve good purposes. They use their knowledge of plants and spirits to improve human existence on earth. Music and speech are considered potent forces in the secret societies because they are phenomena of the invisible world. We cannot see them, yet their impact on us can be profound.

THOSE WHO REFUSE THE MASTER

Komo Society

The Komo secret society is the first one into which the Minianka men can be initiated. It trains the initiates to be masters of the word, for constructive or destructive purposes, as needed. Komo initiates learn their own mastery of fire different from the fire initiation; blacksmiths originally came out of this society. The Komo initiates develop knowledge of the bush and its plants, and they delve into the hidden aspects of music. This was the specialization of my grandfather, who was a Komo initiate.

Komo musicians may witness feats involving mastery of natural phenomena outside the range of normal human capacity. Regardless of what they see in front of them, they must not be astounded. They need to play calmly; a large crowd should cause them no nervousness. They learn through experience not to be influenced by externals. Another important study for Komo initiates is the effect of sound vibrations on the human mind.

The speed and skill of the Komo dancers is remarkable. They claim that spirits have given them knowledge of plants whose use facilitates their prowess in dance. When dancers are feeling fatigued and aching all over their bodies, the Komo initiates give herbal potions to make the dancing easy again.

There are different levels of initiation in the Komo society. The higher initiates cultivate magical powers. During ceremonies, the younger initiates are warned that if they start to hallucinate from the effects of the plants they have ingested or the music they are listening to, they should go home to sleep. Otherwise, they risk becoming mentally unbalanced.

Some young Canadian volunteers went to Mali and met my brother. They said they wanted to see something of the Komo secret society. "That requires rituals," my brother answered, "and besides, it is secret. If you want to talk with people, that is something else, but don't expect to see anything."

The elders did not trust the Canadians to keep silent about things that must be kept secret. They argued with the elders that they would never tell anyone else what they saw. The elders were not convinced and said, "Your intention is sincere now, but you have not been trained, and one day, if you are tempted, you will lose your resolve and speak." The Canadians persisted, and were eventually accepted, with reservations, and had to buy the required chicken.

Despite their reservations, the elders felt that out of courtesy to my brother and me as hosts of these foreigners they would try to show something. "We are soon to pass from this world. The world belongs to the young now."

That night when the Komo drums first sounded, the public spaces were cleared of all the noninitiates at lightning speed, and the Komo participants filled the square. The Canadians were there. The dance began. At a certain point, the elders said, "It is starting to smell bad here." That means that there will soon be corpses here; people will see things they will not be able to endure. In this context, to die means to lose oneself, to hallucinate, to become mentally disturbed.

Hearing the elders' warning, my younger brother told the Canadians to go to bed, but they refused. An enormous baobab tree stood in the square. One Komo initiate charged at it full speed and appeared on the other side. The Canadians were asked, "Did you see that man run?" "Yes," they answered. "Was that the speed of a normal man?" "No." "Did he go through the baobab, around it, or over it?" The Canadians could not answer, they asked, "How was that done?" "This is not a time for your questions, but for you to go to bed."

The Komo musicians and dancers all left the square to accompany the foreigners back to their lodgings with music to make sure they would go. But one Canadian stayed out. Suddenly he was overcome with fear and screamed, "Fire, the whole village is surrounded by fire." Throughout the night he trembled and was unable to sleep. He had been warned; these are not things with which you play around. When you are told it is time for you to go to bed, you don't argue. A Komo musician who later played for the Canadians said he felt blocked in his hands, and that the dance steps did not flow normally either.

Naho Society

Another secret society in Minianka villages, called Naho, is made up of hunters. According to Naho rules, one hunting experience qualifies a villager to join in their dances.

THOSE WHO REFUSE THE MASTER

First, there is a dance for those who have only killed rats. Then, hunters who have shot turtledoves with their arrows can dance. Other dances are for those who have killed a rabbit, a deer. A hunter who has already killed an elephant will not lower himself to join in dances for the killers of smaller animals. A saying among the hunters is, "Don't waste a bullet that can kill an elephant on a rabbit." In ascending order, the killing of panthers, lions, and elephants accords the highest status. The steps of each dance are varied, as are the rhythms. The gestures correspond to the movements of the animals in question. The musicians must be good observers of these animals so that their playing can appropriately follow the dancers.

Niewoh Society

Because my mother is the leader of the Niewoh society, I can speak a bit about it. Their statue is kept in my mother's home. I grew up with it without knowing it was there. It was only in 1982, when my mother saw that I was interested in the mysteries of music and seriously studying how to heal with it, that she showed the statue to me. When my mother dies, another woman will take her place, and I will no longer have access to that knowledge.

All girls are initiated into the Niewoh society by undergoing the excision ceremony, in which the clitoris is surgically removed. After that, they go through a preparation for childbirth. The Niewoh women's society prepares the young women for childbirth and for understanding a mother's role and the sense of self-sacrifice for a child. For example, they teach women ways in which to save a marriage for the sake of a child.

This society is based on the protection of children. It intervenes so that evil spirits do not interfere with the child at birth. It also helps widows who are haunted by the spirits of their deceased husbands. It teaches wives how to subdue violent or recalcitrant husbands. Women come to the Niewoh society to confess their sins as part of the cure for infertility.

The society has a festival every year. The women work in the fields to raise money for their festival and for expenses incurred when they initiate other women into the society. They hire players of the balafon and of the talking drum. When they dance, the men

Figure 4. The fetish statue of the women's Niewoh secret society, alongside a smaller statue.

must go to bed because they are not allowed to participate in the ceremony. This is respected.

The Niewoh music is very important to me.* It is the first music I felt, for I was in the womb when my mother danced at the ceremonies. I grew up in the Niewoh ambiance without knowing the details. Sometimes at night when I was young, I pretended to be asleep and heard the women speaking softly about things I was not supposed to hear. Out of respect for my mother, I will never tell these things to anyone.

In fact, there are many things in our culture that should not be explained. If someone goes to our village and sees something related to the secret societies, I do not feel it is my job to answer questions about the meaning of it. If the person is serious, he or she can inquire about how to be initiated to learn of these things. Words alone do not convey the meaning. The music and the

---

*For music of the Niewoh secret society, listen to "Niewah Yati" on *The Healing Drum* audiocassette (see page 213 for ordering information).

gestures of dance also impart meaning. One should not be content with intellectual explanations alone.

An outsider with a sincere attitude can be integrated deeply into the Minianka culture. In fact, the foreigner is judged according to the same criteria of character as the villagers themselves. I know a French anthropologist who has been almost completely transformed. He participates in our ceremonies. Many elders of our tribe fear him, as he is reputedly a powerful sorcerer. Because of his manner of behaving, his dedication, his willingness to make personal sacrifices, he has learned many things that I myself may never have the opportunity to learn. Over the past twenty years, I have lived mostly in Canada and come back to Fienso for only a month at a time. This anthropologist has stayed in the villages for extended periods. He has devoted much time to learning from the elders, and they have reciprocated generously with him. Anyone who came to the village to learn for a short time would be better off staying at home. Such a person would be given no instruction in the same way a villager who showed impatience and failed to listen carefully would be ignored.

Nia Society

A woman may come to a secret society to ask them to pray for her and to tell the ancestors that she needs a certain child to be sent to her. When the child is born, the society is considered the godparent, and the child belongs to the society as a birthright.

I am linked by birthright to the men's secret society called Nia. The Nia society is concerned with music, communicating with the ancestors, predicting future events, and other matters that must remain secret.* Before my birth, my mother asked the elders of this society to intercede with the ancestors so that an ancestral spirit would be sent to be born through her. The Nia elders performed their ceremony at a spring from the river that flows near my childhood home in Fienso. They approached the ancestors through water and spirits of water. Therefore, I am by temperament of the aquatic type, a man of the water.

---

*For music of the Nia secret society, listen to "Nia Yati" on *The Healing Drum* audiocassette (see page 213 for ordering information).

INITIATIONS AND SECRET SOCIETIES

The name the Nia elders bestowed upon me is Sekie. It means "the one who knows the serious side of reality." Through divination, which is something I know little about, the Nia elders verified my aquatic temperament and more about my individual characteristics.

Not all people come through the medium of water. We believe others come through trees, stones, doors, lion's tails, the sacred wood, or from the ancestors directly.

I have a ritual to observe in relation to my origins: I must sacrifice a white chicken every year at the site of the spring where the elders issued their petition to the ancestors for my birth. If I cannot be at the spring annually, I still renew the ritual when I go to Fienso.

Because of my aquatic temperament, I am very influenced by the full moon. Living in Montreal as I do now, I rarely see the moon directly. Yet when I find myself irritable and in a bad mood, I look at the calendar and see that, sure enough, it is the full moon or just a couple of days before it. If the moon affects someone this way, he or she is probably aquatic.

Maniah Society

The last secret society I shall speak of is called Maniah. My maternal grandfather belonged to this association of warriors. In the past, they were very tough. When the warriors returned from winning a war, they made a human sacrifice of a vanquished warrior. They also brought at least ten men from the losing side to work in the village. Although no longer involved in warfare, the Maniah society still has important ritual functions in village life. They have two huts in the village for their sacrificial rituals. One is square. Nearby is a straw-covered lean-to with a small round hut that has no roof but simply an earthenware pot over it. During their ceremony, the Maniah fetish is brought out of one of these huts and taken around the village three times, accompanied by music.*

During the seven days of the Maniah observance, with its continuous drumming, the men involved are allowed no sexual contact with women. They gather plants in the forest and try to make

---

*For music of the Maniah secret society, listen to "Maniah Yati" on *The Healing Drum* audiocassette (see page 213 for ordering information).

contact with other spirits. All the villagers may enter into the popular celebration when the fetish is carried around the village. Usually one or more women enter a trance state.

Social Regulation by Secret Societies

One role of the secret societies is the protection of their members. If one of the children born into the Nia society, for example, becomes mentally disturbed, the society convenes the entire village by night to determine if the illness has resulted from sorcery. Anyone who did not come to the assembly would be suspect. All those gathered have to confess to any wrongs they have committed regarding the Nia child in question. Someone in trance will say, "I know the guilty party. You had better make peace. Otherwise, you are warned that you will be eliminated." This threat draws forth confessions.

I remember such a gathering of the Nia society from my childhood. The atmosphere was so intense that I myself felt guilty. I thought, perhaps it's me. These phenomena are no longer common practice as the government has been discouraging them. If one of their children died, and they suspected sorcery, the Nia society carried out a similar investigation. They played their drums; some members went into a trance, ran through the village, and cried out, as they sought to find out whether a sorcerer was the cause of the death.

One of the roles of the secret societies is to protect the people from evil spirits. For example, the hunters believe that evil spirits can disguise themselves as animals to lure hunters to their deaths. Likewise, the fishermen believe that some apparent fish are not really fish but spirits. The secret societies of these occupational groups specialize in developing the means to counteract such dangers and to cure people who have been hurt by these spirits.

The secret societies are powerful agents of social regulation and control in the village. They discipline the wider society and seek to eliminate evil once it has been detected. The fear the secret societies can evoke is considered necessary for keeping order among those for whom moral precepts alone would not suffice.

Someone who bears a grudge against another is not expected by the Minianka to become well disposed to his enemy out of his own good will alone. Because of the unknown powers they can employ, the secret societies often act as a deterrent for those with malevolent intentions. No single individual is permitted the delusion of thinking he is stronger than the whole community or that he can violate its interests with impunity. An evildoer will not be able to outwit all of the secret societies. If one secret society fails to uncover a source of disharmony in the community, others will be called into service. Each one has its secrets, its techniques. The Minianka maintain that the good of the society requires elements of social control that instill fear by invoking secret powers to keep people from transgressing moral laws. In my own case, I do not know what the secret societies did after I was shot, and it was never discussed with me later.

Some of the musical instruments played by the secret societies in their rituals have never been seen or even described to the uninitiated. In the village, the sounds of these instruments may be heard, but most of the villagers cannot imagine what sort of instrument produces them. Such mysteries add to the societies' power of persuasion in the community. Initiates into the secret societies know that there are higher levels of initiation with still other secrets to be learned by those who qualify. No individual can consider himself above all the levels. No one can go to the highest level in all the secret societies. This structure acts as a system of checks and balances in community politics.

The men's and women's societies also balance each other. If a man claimed to know all the secrets of the men's societies, he would still be vulnerable to the women's societies, and they could bring him down. It would not be desirable, from the Minianka point of view, for any individual to have access to all the powers and knowledge in the culture. Such a person could become too dangerous to the common interests. Everyone needs something unknown to get on his nerves a bit, to humble him, to make him fear a higher power. The secret societies play this role in Minianka culture.

This discussion of the secret societies reveals the complexity and high degree of organization of a Minianka village. It has happened at times that a person with training in social work, rural development, or psychiatry has been sent by the government to "organize" a village without any adequate orientation about village realities. One such person arrived in Fienso and announced the intention of organizing all the women. When I heard this, my heart trembled. I thought, "They are already organized in secret societies, but they are not going to tell you about it." The village women knew nothing of her diploma or what it was supposed to represent. They saw her as an unmarried girl who still smelled of her mother's milk, and who could not understand their needs. Anyone who wants to work in the village must work through the structures that are already there. When my grandfather was appointed as administrative chief, the only way he could be effective was to win the support of all the sorcerers and sorceresses.

The secret societies are interwoven into the fabric of Minianka culture. They are important here because their musicians have enriched Minianka music and contributed to the cultural resources for overcoming mental and spiritual distress. More about their music and ceremonies follows in Part Two.

PART TWO

THE
HEALING
DRUM

INTRODUCTION

In the Minianka villages of Fienso and Zangasso, the musicians were healers, the healers musicians. The word musician itself implies the role of healer. From the Minianka perspective, it is inconceivable that the responsibilities for making music and restoring health should be separate, as they are in the West.

In the Miniankan view and practice of music, harmony is the central concept—the fitting combination and pleasing interaction of parts in a whole. The encompassing whole for our present purposes is the Minianka cosmos, with its invisible and visible dimensions. The entire Minianka village social structure and culture seek to sustain the lives of the people in harmony with one another, the Creator, the ancestors, the spirits of the bush, and nature. Kle-kolo, the path of the Creator, is the path of harmony. Weaknesses of human character, such as envy, jealousy, and hatred, are sources of disharmony. They cause people to stray from Kle-kolo, set people against one another, and make them vulnerable to harmful influences from invisible spirits, which can be additional sources of disharmony. This is the cosmos in which Minianka musicians play their instruments and heal.

THE HEALING DRUM

The Minianka understand music as a bridge between the visible and invisible realms. The human voice and musical sounds produced on instruments arise from intentions in the invisible human interior and penetrate to the invisible interior of listeners as well as to the surrounding invisible realm of spirits and ancestors. Music thus can be a potent force for maintaining or restoring human harmony with the cosmos. This is its ultimate purpose in Minianka culture.

The Minianka peasants would not think of tilling, sowing, weeding, or harvesting in their fields without the appropriate musical support and accompaniment. Their music enhances the harmony felt by the workers with their labors and with one another. Quite feasibly, the music enhances the life processes in the crops as well.

In the Minianka tradition, the individual cannot be viewed apart from the social and cosmic context. Living in harmony with one's fellow humans in society and with the ancestors, spirits, and Creator in the invisible realm produces psychological health. Conversely, the disturbed thoughts, emotions, and behavior of an individual result from disturbed relations—most commonly with other people, but often with the ancestors and spirits as well. Psychological illness means being out of harmony, and healing is the means of bringing the individual back into harmonious relation with the world. Because Minianka music serves to sustain or restore social and cosmic harmony, it is in essence a tonic and a remedy, one among several available in the culture for the work of healing.

Minianka music and social structure parallel each other in their complexity and sophistication. The music is polyrhythmic, which means that different rhythms are played simultaneously, with their accentuated patterns often crossing one another rather than being synchronous. By contrast, Western music may have two concurrent rhythms, and, on rare occasions, three. A Minianka orchestra normally plays five or more rhythms in such a way that the overall effect is very harmonious. This rhythmic complexity is blended with corresponding melodic and harmonic complexity. Minianka scales are pentatonic, and repeated melodic phrases are subtly varied.

Minianka dancing embodies and expresses the rhythmic complexity of the music. The head, upper torso, hips, hands, and feet of a dancer may move polyrhythmically. If a dancer moves to the center of the circle in a community dance, a dialogue of music

INTRODUCTION

Figure 5. A dancer leaps in front of the balafon in the village square in Fienso.

and movement ensues between musicians and the dancer. The musicians' rhythms intentionally match the dancer's. The other dancers on the circumference of the circle may dance to any one or any combination of the rhythms being played. Thus, the villagers can express their individuality at the same time they celebrate their community. Music is a force for social cohesion. Villagers are not separated into performers and audience—all are participants to whatever degree they choose.

Music is essential to Minianka existence. In the West, by contrast, music is a luxury, an entertainment. In the Minianka village music is necessary for work, celebration, religious observance, initiation, funerals, and healing. Music and dance are learned in much the same way that we learn to walk or to speak our native language. The Minianka learn to dance by participating from the earliest age in community dancing. Children with an interest in music learn by playing with more experienced players. To play means to be playful as well as to make music.

Women of all ages are also musicians. They sing and play a wide variety of instruments. A special instrument for women is the water drum, which is made from a vessel filled with water and covered with an inverted calabash. The musician beats the calabash to make a beautiful, resonant music. The Niewoh women's society has its own musicians and sometimes invites male musicians to play at some ceremonies.

In the complex Minianka social life, relations among individuals are regulated by various obligations in overlapping social networks: extended and usually polygamous families, age groups, work groups, a neighborhood, a village, and possibly one or more secret societies. The individual is also subject to influences from the ancestors and the spirits of the bush. Living in harmony in the midst of this social and cosmic complexity is a difficult art. Music plays a major role in helping individuals and groups manage the tensions of living in society.

When an individual becomes disturbed, the Minianka look to disturbed relationships as the cause, since psychological imbalance is seen as a symptom of social imbalance and possible disharmony with the invisible world. The Minianka regard their musicians as having the necessary skills of intelligence, memory, observation, and social interaction required to bring a person back into tune with self and others. In their playing, musicians need a sense of harmony, proportion, balance, and social tact so that their interactions with fellow musicians and dancers contribute to the harmony of the whole. Musicians need sensitivity and the ability to respond appropriately to the demands of the moment. Regular accompaniment to dancers attunes musicians to the manifestations of individuality through movement.

Emotional disturbance is expressed in irregularities of muscle tone and blocked, disharmonious neuromuscular and physiological rhythmic processes. An emotionally unbalanced person experiences shallow or irregular breathing, heart symptoms such as tachycardia, functional digestive disturbances, and distressed thinking that is reflected in excited brain wave patterns. Music profoundly affects muscle tone, body rhythms, and emotions; respiration, heartbeat, digestive peristalsis, and brain waves tend to become synchronized to music. By playing appropriate rhythms the Minianka musicians stabilize and synchronize the physiological and motor rhythms of their patients through the audible vibrations of music.

Normal rhythms are synonymous with health. A requisite of Minianka musicianship is that musicians themselves stay relaxed while playing. The musical tones subtly communicate the musicians' own optimal muscle tone to the patient, whose musculature will be influenced toward balanced tone as well.

When fellow villagers make music to heal a psychologically disturbed patient, the musicians enter into harmony with the patient. This is a socializing initiative that overcomes alienation and is a step toward empowering the patient to enter into harmony with society. Music also touches the depths of human emotions in an immediate and powerful way. Thus, the Minianka musicians can facilitate emotional release for their fellows who are suffering from emotional blockage or turmoil.

The nightly dancing in the village square provides all villagers with tonifying physical, psychological, social, and spiritual renewal. The physical benefits include the release of tensions, lubrication of joints and muscles, and enhancement of neuromuscular coordination. On this level, Minianka village dancing plays the role that sports and fitness training do in the West. Psychologically, the villagers enjoy the freedom of playfully expressing themselves, the pleasure of rhythmical movement, the release of emotional pressures, and the temporary departure from the worries and hardships of survival. Socially, they are united with one another and their ancestors in response to the music of the drum and balafon. As its vibrations reverberate into the invisible realm, the music quickens awareness of the spiritual mystery of life, and the dancing expresses the vitality of life. That is why dance is a great preventive remedy for the Minianka.

Trance

Trance is an integral part of traditional Minianka rituals. In a state of trance, the individual loses normal self-awareness. The Minianka say that a spirit has mounted the individual's body and temporarily displaced the person's double. Trances do not usually occur during the secular dances of communal celebration. They are intentionally induced only during the ceremonies of the secret, initiatory societies. As in other cultures where trance is a part of religious ritual, the entranced Minianka speak in tongues, that is, in strongly metered utterances incomprehensible to the average person. These utterances require interpretation by special initiates and are held to be messages from the invisible world.

THE HEALING DRUM

Cross-cultural studies have shown a remarkable consistency in the actual sound of glossolalia, which seems to have nothing to do with the native language of the speakers. Interpretations of the utterances, however, *are* culturally specific. In all cases where trance and glossolalia are known to occur, they are socially validated, ritualistically induced, and meaningful within the cultural context. Social scientists have interpreted trance, glossolalia, and spirit possession as ways of empowering people through contact with the spirit realm, releasing deep tensions, validating belief systems, coping with social stresses, and getting authorization from invisible sources for difficult decisions.

As a boy, Yaya fled from elder musicians who were making music known to induce trances. He has never been in a trance, nor does it attract him. He refrains from playing rhythms that are trance inducing. Yaya is concerned with music that can help people to function as more conscious, balanced, self-possessed human beings.

When the dance and music of the Minianka or other African tribes are taught in the West, their original social and historical context deserves to be taught along with them. As we have seen, Minianka music and dance are integral parts of a complex cultural whole. Aesthetic principles are but one aspect of this whole. Perhaps the growing appeal of African music and dance in the West is only partly due to the sheer exuberance and joie de vivre they often express. Beyond that, they may bear a message about communal solidarity, about caring, healing, and sharing in the joys and sorrows of life together, about getting back into harmony with ourselves, one another, and our world. This is a message that we in the West, along with modern Africans, need to listen to as we suffer breakdowns of community, family, morality, and our ecological base on earth. African music and dance, in addition to being fun, may stir in us some nascent awareness of a humane, down-to-earth solidarity that has been lost in our mechanized culture and that we need to rediscover.

Dancing symbolizes the rhythmic, patterned movements of life itself. Music and dance amplify and make manifest to our senses the unheard tones and unseen waves that weave together the matter of existence. Even when we are sitting most still or resting in deepest sleep, the atoms, molecules, cells, tissues, organs, and systems of our bodies dance in astounding harmony and exchange

INTRODUCTION

ambient energies from air, water, food, and invisible electromag-
netic radiation. The beat, the rhythm, the timing, the orchestration, the flow, the balance between action and rest must all be
within well-defined, organic limits for us to be vital. The Minianka
practice a healing art that helps restore emotionally and psychologically disturbed people to harmonious human functioning through
appropriately pulsating music.

MUSICAL
INSTRUMENTS

I **received my first drum** thanks to an accident when I was about five years old. The story starts when a huge fromager tree fell down for a reason I do not remember. The fromager is almost as big as our biggest tree, the baobab, and is closely related to it. Its wood is soft and white. One tree provides abundant wood for many stools, bowls, plates and other things. Consequently, when this tree fell down, a blacksmith of our village who was also a skilled woodworker carried his hatchet and adze out to the tree and worked right there fashioning useful things for the village.

One afternoon I went out to watch him work. He was my uncle, my father's brother, and in the same age group as my father, so I was related to him and could talk with him freely. When he finished his day's work, I offered to carry one of his tools home for him. He gave me a wooden-handled adze, which I slung over one shoulder, handle in front and blade resting over my back. I walked proudly with his tool. Then I slipped and fell. The adze cut into my upper back.

"You are going to have to pay me for this," I said to the blacksmith.

Figure 6. A baobab tree.

"How do you want me to pay you?" he asked.

"With this tool, you are going to carve a small drum for me."

He agreed. His other work took priority, though, and he did not finish the drum immediately. Each day I went to his workshop and demanded my drum. Finally, he carved it and gave it to me. When the other children of my age group saw my drum, they all wanted to have one like it. They insisted and insisted. The blacksmith produced them, and the children were content. The blacksmith joked that he used to make useful things like stools and bowls, but now he was making useless things, little drums for young boys.

Seeing my age mates with their drums gave me the idea of forming my first orchestra.

I was six years old, and there were ten boys in my orchestra. Each one of us had a little drum, and we played the same piece over and over again. Although we played a lot, we made no progress. I directed everything and insisted they play what I told them. There were musically gifted boys among them, but if they played better than I did, they had a fight on their hands. I would not tolerate it. I told them that if they did not do as I indicated the fight with me would not end in a day so they had better not start anything.

My elder, Nangape, was aware of what was going on. Without saying anything to me, he sent a fifteen-year-old musician from his orchestra. The big boy challenged us and asked if that was all we knew how to play. I argued that what we did was very good and certainly sufficient. He told me to shut up, sit down, and give him my drum. He produced sounds from it that I had not even known were possible. The others took it all in.

When the more advanced player left, I challenged my orchestra, "Are you happy with that? If so, let me know, and we will fight right away."

In my depths, I was very unhappy. I enlisted the services of my little sister. While I played with my group and imitated the way the elders played, she kept a lookout. When the boy who had shown me up came along, she warned us. We ran. I did not want him to give another demonstration. All ten of us hid out in my mother's hut and drummed there. She soon told us to go play outside. I sent my sister again to see if the older boy was around.

MUSICAL INSTRUMENTS

This scenario was replayed many times, and I somehow convinced myself that we were great musicians until the day my mother cried out, "Stop. This noise is going to kill me."

"So, we are not so good after all," I reflected. If I was going to kill my mother with my music, how good could it be? I still had things to learn and should let the others play a little too. Nangape finally told me he had sent his musician to wake me up because I was brutalizing the other boys with my insistence on being the best.

For people of my tribe, with its rich musical context, exposure to music begins in the womb, when pregnant mothers join in the community dances. From inside the womb, our babies feel the vibrations of the rhythms enter their bodies. Infants are then wrapped onto their mothers' backs with a cloth and taken into the dancing circle with everyone else. Children are included in community celebrations and hear the same music as the adults. Our children are welcome to participate at any age.

The first toy given to a child by a Minianka mother is usually a little balafon, drum, or bell. This shows the honored place of music in our culture. Training to play an instrument is introduced without any forcing. Any child—male or female—who wishes may learn to make music. We do not have a caste of musicians, as do some other tribes, such as the Mandingo in Mali. Certain families are, however, the traditional guardians of particular instruments. The care of teaching music is transmitted from father to son in these families. Nangape's family are guardians of the n'peenyee, and it must be housed in their compound. Playing it is of necessity taught through this family.

No one is forbidden to play music, but not just anyone is permitted to play just anything at any time. Certain melodies and rhythms attract the spirits, and only a special category of initiated people may play this music. When young and inexperienced balafonists and flutists are practicing, the elders burn certain plants to offset the bad effects of the music. The odor of those burning plants is not a compliment to the players, but it may give them some protection until they can make music that has a safe and wholesome effect on the environment.

Our musicians play to bring well-being to the entire human, natural, and spiritual community. Beyond pleasing people with our playing, we need to communicate with the invisible world.

Figure 7. Women dance in front of a balafon in the Fienso village square.

Musical instruments, known as *yatinyi,* are likewise respected for their power to derange or heal. That is why our musicians' apprenticeships must be long and demanding.

The Balafon

The balafon is considered an instrument of the spirits, of the invisible world, of the inner dimensions. Sometimes called the African xylophone, the balafon is a melodious instrument indigenous to West Africa. Carved wooden keys are mounted on a rectangular wooden frame. Strung underneath the frame are a series of gourds with holes cut into their tops—these act as resonators. The musician hits the keys with two sticks wrapped with rubber on the ends. Its tones have a quality that resonates with the water element in the abdominal center of the human body and with atmospheric water such as rain.[*] At the same time, the balafon could be consid-

---

[*]For balafon music, listen to "Warizie" on *The Healing Drum* audiocassette (see page 213 for ordering information).

ered a kind of wind instrument because of the air that moves through the gourds.

The balafon was probably descended from ancient Stone Age instruments similar to those still played today in Togo. Oral tradition recounts stories of hunter-gatherer groups who heard different tones in the rocks they chipped into tools. The people lined up rocks according to size and played them to hear the pleasant sounds they made.

Subsequently, they experimented by digging holes in the ground, laying wooden boards across the holes, and striking the boards to make music. The resulting sounds gave the impression of coming from an inner space, as if from the interior of the human body, or from the earth itself.

According to legend, the balafon in its present form was revealed by a spirit to a man named Sumanguru Kantey. He saw the balafon and heard its music in his dreams, awoke, and made the first one. Sumanguru Kantey lived in the tenth century. He was a king of the Sousou tribe, who dwell on the coast of West Africa in what is now the Republic of Guinea. Use of the instrument spread to other tribes.

Among the Minianka, the balafon is used for all religious ceremonies that establish contact with the invisible world. It is essential for funeral music and for the ceremony of the sacred wood. The balafon is understood to attract spirits. When the balafon and reed flute are played together, their tonal vibrations also strongly affect creatures without an outer ear. Reptiles, including poisonous snakes, are called out of hiding and so people wear shoes on such occasions to protect themselves. Traditional musicians will not play the balafon unless they are wearing protective amulets designed to repel any bad spirits among the many attracted by the music of this sacred instrument.

Bafoko, Djémé, and Tama

The *bafoko* is made of a large calabash covered somewhat loosely by a goatskin. In the middle of it is a circle of resin about four inches in diameter. This spot of dried resin gives a different tone from the rest of the skin when it is hit. The bafoko is widely played in ceremonies and accompanies the balafon.

A string instrument called the *bolon* is based on the bafoko. A

Figure 8. Balafon players sit to the right, bafoko players stand to the left in the village square of Fienso.

millet stalk pierces the skin of the bafoko and is attached to the inside of the calabash. Two strings attach to the end of the stalk that rises above the skin and extend to the outside of the calabash. It gives a bass sound when plucked, and it is played at funerals and other ceremonies. The skin amplifies the sound of the strings, and the calabash acts as a resonator.

The *djémé* is a popular drum. People say it originated among the Bambara tribe. It is carved from a tree trunk into a shape like a vase, wider at the top, narrower at the bottom, and has a goatskin head. In principle, the drum has three tones, but it takes quite a while to produce them correctly. Once the tones are mastered, different rhythms can be learned. The body of the djémé is hollow and the bottom open; it should never be blocked by placing it on the ground since that muffles the sound. The drum is usually suspended from two straps, one around each shoulder, so the musician can move around while playing. One reason the djémé is tapered is to fit more easily between the drummer's legs.

The musician is very particular about his drum—often he negotiates with the woodcarver who will make the drum body for him

MUSICAL INSTRUMENTS

Figure 9. A player of the talking drum, tama, at a village celebration in Fienso.

to be sure it suits his needs. He may even go with the carver to select the precise tree from which the djémé is to be fashioned. The larger djémé can be fairly heavy, but the drummer is accustomed to moving about freely with this portable drum and is not bothered by its weight. Like the bafoko, the djémé is a hand drum. No sticks or other tools are used in playing it. The djémé is often used for playing work music.

The *tama* is another popular drum in my culture. Americans call this a talking drum, but in my tribe we only play music on it. We are happy to talk with words and do not need drums for our conversations. The tama drum is small, carved from a tree trunk, and shaped like an hourglass, wider at both ends and narrow in the middle. It too is completely hollow. Both ends are covered with lizard skin and laced together with leather cords that are themselves important parts of the instrument. The tama is slung over the left shoulder with a strap and held close to the armpit. The player's upper arm squeezes and releases the cords, thereby changing the tension on the drum head, which is hit with the fingers of the left hand and a small curved wooden drumstick held in the right hand. The tonal qualities of the tama are subtle and varied due to the player's ability to change the tension of the cords. The tama is so portable that it is used for all sorts of music.

Rhythms

When we play the drums, sometimes we learn complex rhythms with the help of phrases that we repeat aloud or in our minds. It is fun, and we laugh about it. An example is "Y siridurouta fla burouta." Besides being a mnemonic to help us recall the rhythm, the phrase is a moral reminder as well. It means, "If you want to have a chief, start a bad habit." This is a traditional Minianka teaching, pointing to the fact that the most tyrannical force in a person's life is his or her own bad habit. It can come to dominate worse than a political leader. When a person is addicted to cigarettes, for example, he or she cannot do without them. One can be living in the most democratic country in the world but still feel driven to leave the house at four in the morning in the worst weather in search of a cigarette. Freedom is gone under the domination of the bad habit. Our songs are vehicles of wisdom teaching. If the amusing combination of sounds makes us laugh while practicing the rhythms, so much the better. Meanwhile, the teaching is also reinforced.

One song that I often perform in concert states, "You do not have to perform acts of charity to benefit your society. Become yourself one less problem to your parents and neighbors, and this will be your greatest gift." Naturally, the translation cannot reproduce the rhythms, rhymes, and plays on words of the original. The important point here is that in my culture art is allied with morality.

THE MINIANKA MUSICIAN'S
APPRENTICESHIP

In **Minianka society,** the musicians are expected to live by high standards of morality and self-restraint. Music is powerful. By their example, the musicians will influence the youth for better or worse. As the youth are the society's future, it is very important that their role models be good ones. The fundamental principle of Minianka musical training is devotion to music in the service of the cosmos, the environment, and the community.

The Teacher

The youth who wants to learn to play an instrument well must choose a music teacher, called "the father who sharpens my hand for the instrument." The elder Nangape was my teacher. The child may come to respect this new father even more than his actual biological father. The apprentice musician will do everything he can for his mentor: help around his home, gather firewood, find termites for his chickens, fetch water. He looks up to his teacher, observes his moral behavior, and follows him closely. If provoked, the older musician might get annoyed and slap the boy from time to time. This is not taboo in the village, nor is a blow from a stick. The musical apprenticeship is not always easy.

I know the case of one young man who wanted to become a musician. He approached an elder, a master musician, to receive training. The elder invited him to stay and work in his family. The young man performed every labor he was asked, including working in the fields. The old master never once spoke with him about music or invited him to sit next to the drum while he played.

At the end of three years, the elder summoned the apprentice and asked him, "Why are you here at my home?"

"I have come to learn to play the drum," the young man answered.

"Then take a drum and play," said the old man.

"Gladly," said the apprentice. He took a drum and played.

"You hear that?" said the master. "It is not necessary for me to teach you. You may leave now. Goodbye."

The young man was ready. He had been exposed to enough fine playing in the three years. He had observed well because of his sincere intention. By the quality of sounds produced, the master knew his apprentice was fit to be on his own as a musician. A master, in fact, can hear one tap on the drum by a younger musician and know the quality of playing to expect. One tap suffices for auditioning musicians to play in a ceremony.

The musical father, however, is basically a protector of the child. When a young musician chooses his teacher, it means that, although very young, the boy may be a member of his teacher's orchestra. When they play, he sits there but does not play himself. He listens and observes for at least a year. Just to say that he belongs to a musical group is a privilege for him. During the second year, he is allowed to touch his instrument. He marks the beat with a stick against the drum. That is all he is permitted to do, but it is not an easy task to accomplish while others are doing complex solos.

This stage of his training can last for two, three, or four years. By listening and observing, he is sharpening his senses through practice. One day the boy is told that he will play a given instrument. After holding the steady beat of the metronome, he takes up a second drum, if he is learning drums, and then one instrument at a time in order of increasing difficulty. Finally he has the entire orchestration in mind from metronome to solo.

THE MINIANKA MUSICIAN'S APPRENTICESHIP

Along with technical training, the young musician must learn how to listen to advice and to be available for what is required of him. He will be subjected to tests. If his musical father observes that the apprentice is of a fearful disposition, he may wake the boy at four in the morning and demand that he go to the cemetery. This is to verify whether the musical aspirant has conquered his fear. A fearful musician would not be very useful to the society. Like a doctor in the West, a Minianka musician might be called upon in the darkest hours of the night for his services. He does not learn to play music for himself but to help the community.

Effects of Sound

Throughout a musical apprenticeship, you need to be conscious that you are emitting sounds and that these sounds have an impact on people. You see it when you play music and people cry in response to some sounds and dance in response to others. If you play in a sloppy way, people will say, "Oh no, not that," and they will behave more nervously. As you play, you see many things like this. You do not need anyone to tell you about it if you pay attention to what is happening.

In relation to music, human beings are strange animals. They go into a room, make some sounds they call music, and enjoy themselves moving around, which they call dancing. Just because of some noise they move. They cry, too, and get excited because of sounds. Some of them spend their time planning what kind of sounds to make. Others become so attached to only one kind of music that they refuse to listen to any other sort.

If such reactions to music are so evident to our eyes, how much more does music affect our health and minds. This kind of realization is not taught: you observe and live these things. When you are playing music, you need to be conscious of how you are affecting people. I have met many musicians in North America who want only to make a hit record, regardless of the value of the music on deeper levels. They are not aware of the subtle effects of music on human well-being, but musicians should be aware of their role. They can build or destroy. They can produce tears, fatigue, excitement, or calm in people. None of my teachers in Fienso taught me about it with words; I learned this from experience. Playing music to benefit the people was the fundamental value of our musical culture.

Discretion is a prime virtue for the musician. When the community does not want to hear music, he must stop playing. If, for example, his music were to disturb workers at their labors, that would be a violation of its reason for existing. Self-restraint is the watchword. Training aims to reduce the ego. Knowing how to produce sounds is only one aspect of musical training. Recognizing the reactions of people and of the visible and invisible worlds is a second aspect of even higher priority.

Musician and Dancer

In the Minianka culture, the musician follows the dancers. The dancers move, and the musician finds the corresponding sounds. It is a dialogue. Visible waves of body movement speak and are answered by audible waves of music. The dialogue continues. Sometimes it becomes a debate, a competition. The musician is evaluated on the basis of his ability to follow movements and gestures spontaneously. A person dances. The musician is not able to follow. The dancer is discontented and insinuates the musician knows nothing. If his ego is centered on solo improvisations, the player will not be appreciated. To improvise is to follow dancers.

Each dancer is unique, so each improvisation will be unique. A musician who follows a good dancer is inspired by the varied movements. His music will be graced with more variety, but not just for variety's sake. The musician who sits down alone to create solos does not benefit from this dynamic, varied interchange. The Minianka musician's art is to know the impact of sound on the body, to read the gestures of the dancer, and to interpret them on his drum. The dancer in turn hears the sounds and interprets them through movement.

When I was rehearsing a group of dancers and musicians in North America, one day some countrymen from Mali arrived. They had been told that an African was playing music for dancers. At their request, I agreed to play for them. One of the women was a powerful dancer with fluid, subtle movement. She had not expected to find a musician who was trained like me in America. She became excited and wanted to show the virtuosity of our Malian culture in music and dance, so she danced all the more joyously and vigorously. I followed her with my playing but lost some of the orchestra since they had not been trained in this way. I told some of the musicians to stop playing and, at least, to observe. I continued to follow the dancers.

During the performance, I produced sounds that had not previously been under my control. I didn't know I was capable of playing like that, mastering things I didn't know I could. I followed the dancer, and my music became more varied.

Observation

When the egocentric preoccupations of the apprentice are sufficiently reduced through training, the apprentice is ready to cultivate knowledge. The Minianka musician must become an observer who looks and feels.

In the Minianka view, a person's identity is expressed in the way he or she dances; dancing reveals one's character. Mediocrity, refinement, nobility, aggression—whatever is present in the individual—shows clearly in the dancing. An arrogant person may be doing the same step as everyone else but dances as if challenging others. An incoherent person may be seen here and there around the dance space, with no cohesion in his or her movements. One can already conclude that an attempt at conversation with this person would prove futile. Vain people dance a bit and look around to see if others have been looking at them. They are not concentrating on the dancing itself but on the impression they are making. When sexually disturbed people dance, their movements make allusion to sexuality and sensuality. Their dance may reveal their fantasies, or their preoccupations with qualities lacking in their lives. Others may be unresolved as to their sexual orientation, whether heterosexual or homosexual. This shows in their dancing. Dancing can also reveal a man's conflict about his potency, without his being aware of it.

A careful observer can read much in the way people dance. The Minianka musicians are trained to note the significance of small gestures and tensions as well as big movements and thereby enter into contact with the invisible aspects of the people in front of them.

Because so much of our dance reflects the movements and gestures performed in our daily occupations, and because we use music to accompany our daily work, the Minianka musician is trained to be an acute observer of all the work performed in the village. These observations occur in a natural, unobtrusive way. No teacher imposes an obligation on the young musician to watch work being performed. Rather, the conviviality of village life and the mutual interest the people take in one another's means of livelihood ensure that all musicians will see the working rhythms and movements of their fellow villagers. A Minianka village is very open. No work is hidden from the public eye or enclosed in an inaccessible private space such as a factory.

The musicians are, of course, workers themselves. They must toil for their own subsistence. No systematic study of work gestures is necessary. Informal contacts in daily life provide ample occasion for a musician to chat with the blacksmith beside the latter's forge or with a rope maker as he twists and braids fibers into serviceable cords. When the weaver sits at his horizontal loom and pushes his shuttle back and forth, he welcomes conversation. The workers are not distracted by human company. To the contrary, fellowship helps speed the work along. Knowing they will enjoy the privilege of playing for their neighbors' dancing, the musicians watch the work they come across with an alert and purposeful eye.

Memory

Each instrument is considered a universe to be discovered rather than mastered, and the apprentice needs to work with it patiently and to feel in no hurry. His mentor also must be patient. Music must be learned thoroughly, as it is not acceptable to say, "I forgot." Some music is played only once a year. Among the Dogon tribe in Mali, for example, some music is played on a sixty-year cycle. Because there is no organized daily practice, once the musician has learned a particular type of music, he must remember it. For example, much music involves short repeated rhythmical phrases, and on the day of a ceremony, these rhythmic combinations will be repeated over and over. A young musician will have ample opportunity to memorize music that is new to him. The music then must be nourished within him, and he may practice by listening to it inwardly without touching an instrument or producing a sound. Later, at the appropriate moment, he plays it.

THE MINIANKA MUSICIAN'S APPRENTICESHIP

Genealogy is another branch of musical studies. The apprentice learns the history of each family, of the spirits, the trees, the animals. Musicians are also the keepers of the cosmological lore of our people. During the village dances and during work music, family lineage is eulogized through songs; the musician needs to be a good singer, too.

The musician also needs to know each person's character. During community dances, when someone moves into the center of the circle, the musicians sound a friendly warning about his or her traits and temperament. In my case, the musicians sing, "When you are Yaya's friend, you have the best friend in the world. When you become his enemy, he is the worst enemy on earth." Each villager has some defining characteristic. About my father, the musicians sing, "If you listen to him, he will get you mixed up in trouble; he will take you in."

Healing

If the musician decides to enter deeply into the domain of healing, his training becomes even longer. No formalized grading establishes distinctions among levels of achievement in such matters, however. When a musician plays, his skill with his instrument speaks for itself. The older, more knowledgeable musicians who notice a younger player's sincere devotion to the art and recognize his potential to be of healing service will point out the uses of various herbs.

This occurs casually. Walking along with a young musician one day, an elder may spot a rare herb. He will say, "Ah, we do not see that very often. I will tell you how to prepare and use it." Similarly, some plants are gathered only when they are in flower. At that time, an elder may take an apprentice out to the bush and instruct him in the lore related to a given plant. No prescribed course or timetable indicates the scope and sequence of what is to be learned; knowledge is transmitted as if by chance. Yet from one generation to the next, the essentials are preserved. I learned what I would call the required minimum of herbal knowledge in just this way.

The musician who practices healing does not have a title to differentiate him from any other musician. In the village community, we know one another's qualifications for any job, whether it is weaving, pottery or healing. Each musician-healer specializes.

Some are concerned with healing mental illness, others can help patients to overcome sexual difficulties through appropriate herbal remedies. Some are conciliators, who intervene skilfully in the quarrels of others and help make peace. We know who is versed in herbal knowledge, observes human behavior keenly, is available any time he is called, and offers his services unselfishly and free of charge.

The patient's family will bring, for example, a red rooster to the musician when engaging his services so that he can barter for any materials needed for the healing. If the musical healer is successful, the healed patient will bring him a gift. The nature of the gift depends on the patient's means. No minimum payment is set. The healer and patient know each other. The healer would not want to impose an unfair burden on the patient. Consequently, the healer may request a chicken, a rooster, a robe, or a cow depending on the patient's ability to furnish this item comfortably. If the healer is unsuccessful, he receives no gift.

Killing the Ego

In our musical apprenticeship, we often hear this paradoxical principle: in the craft of music, make your friends your enemies, and your enemies your friends. This is intended to teach the value of criticism. Friends, who only flatter a musician for his playing, do not help him develop his art. They lack discernment. Enemies, that is, critics of his playing, help him to stay humble and to work for improvement. A musical father will work on this aspect of a student's personality to help him become immune to false pride and to remain open to honest criticism. This way an apprentice learns to evaluate criticism for any truth it may contain.

Minianka musicians are deemed worthy of learning new rhythms for higher levels of musical initiation on the basis of their characters as much as their technical proficiency. They cannot pay a price to learn more music or insist that it is their right to do so. It is not a matter of rights but of merit; the attitudes and behavior of the musicians qualify them to pass from one stage to another.

On a visit to Fienso, I went to talk with the elders about music. They questioned me: "What are you doing there in Canada?"

I answered, "I play some music and teach some courses."

"For whom?" they queried.

THE MINIANKA MUSICIAN'S APPRENTICESHIP

I said, "For the past year, I have been taking my drum and balafon into the schools and playing for the children."

They continued to question me: "What do you do with them?"

"I explain to them how our instruments are made. I speak to them. They touch the drum. For me, they are like my children. I enjoy the contact with them. Often I get mail from them. They send me their drawings and letters. Sometimes I even teach six classes a day. From time to time, I give workshops for adults who want to try playing our music. I try to give them a dimension of what we have."

The elders said, "Good. At least you are in the service of something. If you were just playing for playing's sake, it would not interest us. We would have nothing to give you for that."

Sometimes, Westerners go to Africa to improve their drumming skills. They are questioned about their motivation and about the time they have available. When they are in a hurry and motivated to be showmen, they are just given lessons in technique. The Minianka are aware that a technically skilled player can impress a lot of listeners without touching on what is deepest in music. Technique can look and sound impressive to outsiders but lack what is essential within the culture. It has happened that a foreigner is told he will learn from the best teacher. "Best" might merely imply that the teacher in question is the best available to impart technique, not someone who would give of his heart or share his love of the instrument. He might even be someone who does not care much about morality or the higher potentials of music.

The best Minianka musicians do not attract notice. They may even have stopped playing. They may sit quietly and chat about the deeper aspects of music. In front of a group, they may start the song and then let the others continue while they observe, plan, keep the evil spirits in check. They have nothing more to prove in the way of producing sounds. Rapid, dexterous playing fascinates youth but represents only a stage through which a musician passes. For the traditional Minianka, a musical instrument is not an arm of persuasion or intimidation, not a means of showing off or of attracting members of the opposite sex. The player does not have to resemble anyone else, just himself. Playing the instrument should look easy. It is art. The Minianka appreciate a musician who has internalized his skills to the point that he can relax while playing. There should be no strain in his body, no grimaces on his face. Inner concentration, calm, and contentment are preferable.

Aside from a deaf person, there was no one who sang worse than my music teacher, Nangape, yet he taught the chants. He knew so much. He no longer had his singing voice, but he was impressive. He understood things. When he trained me, we went each day to sit under a tree. From there we could hear several people playing music in the village. I didn't know why we went there. I heard fragments of music from here and there. Then one day I said, "Oh, you would think it is an orchestra playing." This was a spot from which all the music around the village could be heard harmoniously. He took me there until I could hear this for myself.

To conclude from the widespread use of music in African culture that all black people are good musicians is an error to be avoided. Music is not in our blood; we need to put it there through practice and training. Our daily life from the earliest years gives us abundant opportunity to assimilate the rhythms, tones, and harmonies of our musical heritage. And that is the subject of the next chapter.

 9

MUSIC, WORK,
AND DANCE

When the Minianka work, they move rhythmically. When they dance, their movements express the activities of daily life. Most popular, traditional dances in Africa are directly related to work, whether they repeat the movements of physical labor or honor different occupations. When people dance in the evening, their movements follow the gestures of the work they have been doing during the day. A fisherman does not dance in the same way as a hunter.

Often the work itself can be seen as a dance. When women wash clothes on the riverbank, they make music by slapping the clothes against the calabashes. To pound grain into daily cereal, four women stand around a large mortar carved out of a portion of tree trunk. Their pestles rise and fall like pistons. The cadence is accentuated by throwing pestles up in the air, clapping hands, and catching the pestles. If one of the women loses the beat, it will break the rhythm of the others. In the blacksmith's workshop, the boy with the bellows sets the first rhythm with a steady in-and-out motion on his accordion-like instrument. The smith hits the metal on the anvil in a second rhythm that makes a musical harmony with the sound of the bellows. Once when the blacksmith's son was ill, I was called in to replace him and use the bellows. I worked hard but didn't pay attention to the rhythm. My production was good, the fire burned brightly, but the smith was accustomed to a different music. Consequently, he could not hit the metal or shape it as he wanted for the job. The beat was off.

When the farmers are breaking ground in the fields with the short-handled hoe known as the *daba,* they follow a particular rhythm. If it is said that one man tills poorly, this is not because he is slower than the rest. Rather, his rhythm is disordered and disturbs the others. When twenty-five people are all turning over the soil in a field, the noise must not be cacophonous. Whatever the work may be, all villagers know not to distract from the group effort with discordant sounds or lack of rhythm.

People do not work alone. To do so is considered suicidal, partly because of dangers such as poisonous snakes and partly because of the psychological effects of isolation. A group of friends unite to do a job together. They know at the outset that they will work at the same speed, eat lunch at the same hour. They must not quarrel during their time of commitment together. No one should be criticized for being slower than the others. The company of each member of the work group is welcome. Even a physically handicapped person has a place. No person's participation should be a source of conflict.

If ten villagers are brought together to work without a musician, nothing will be accomplished. The group chooses a musician to play for them while they work. The productivity of the group depends on the musician who accompanies them. A salary increase could not be as effective. Whipping would only provoke revolt. A good musician behind the group, who follows the rhythm of each member, will help them all to accelerate. His playing will make the work enjoyable, or at least less painful.

Agriculture is the indispensable base of the entire Minianka village economy. Fishermen, hunters, musicians, craftsmen, black-smiths, and any others who specialize in extra activities still maintain their own fields.

The musicians are repaid for their services by having the farmers who were helped come to work an appropriate amount of time on the musician's fields the following day.

MUSIC, WORK, AND DANCE

The months of May, June, and July are the season when the rains begin to fall and the hardest agricultural labors take place. In tilling with the daba the farmers' knees and backs are bent, and the big metal blade turns over a heavy load of soil with each dig into the earth. Without music, this severe toil would be more difficult to bear. A musician-farmer never plays in his own field—he calls in other musicians for that task. This is to preclude any temptation for a musician to push other workers too hard in his field.

Each job has a particular rhythm. In the case of sowing seeds, the musician must know the music that goes with placing the seeds in the earth and stamping the dirt over them. As the movements for weeding are different from those for sowing, naturally the accompanying music must be different also. The harvest too has specific music to facilitate the gathering of the ripe crop. Thus, there is not just one sort of music for the farmers but different sorts depending on the job at hand.

When a group of farmers are working in a field, the musician encourages each one of them individually. He follows one man for at least ten minutes before going on to the next. Moving along behind the laborer, the musician plays rhythms on the drum to warm him up. At the same time, the musician sings of the worker's personal characteristics and genealogy, praises his parents, and enhances his pride in himself. Stimulated in this way, the worker speeds up, and the others follow him. The musician then goes behind another to continue in the same way.* By the end of the day each man's memory has been refreshed about his ancestors' accomplishments and his self-esteem has been boosted. Productivity increases because each worker wants to live up to the ancestral example.

Music and Daily Life

As I said earlier, the Minianka believe that music was created not only for pleasing the ear: it must have a meaning, express an activity, a natural or supernatural force, a feeling. Without mean-

---

*For music played by these drummers at an evening "jam session," listen to "Don" on *The Healing Drum* audiocassette (see page 213 for ordering information).

ing, it loses its reason for being. Music is respected as a powerful force that must be thoroughly appropriate to the occasion.

For strenuous physical work in general, the drum or some other percussion instrument is required. This pushes people to exert themselves, to move. Melodious music, such as that from the flute or violin, would reduce physical productivity by enticing the workers to listen to the beautiful melodies. If a young boy started playing a flute next to some farmers who were working in a field, one of the farmers would politely ask the boy to finish playing elsewhere.

For work involving delicate hand–eye coordination and mental concentration, the drum is an unwelcome accompaniment. Youthful drumming would disconcert the tailor or shoemaker. By learning early in his training to abstain from playing in inappropriate places, the musician consecrates himself to the community.

One instrument, a two-stringed guitar known as the *bolon*, is renowned for its ability to inspire courage. In past times of warfare among the different ethnic groups, bolon players would sing about the community's need to prepare all of the warriors to engage in battle. Tendencies to fear or cowardice were thus overcome. In Mali, stories are told of two musicians, Batrou Sekou and Sidiki Diabate. It is said that the latter played for the warriors right on the battleground, while the former gave them courage in the evening to take up the fight again the next day. The two complemented each other.

In a Minianka village, when a child is born, there is a special drum call. It signals the event and the baby's sex to everyone. There may also be a cry or a rifle shot in the air. At the ceremony for naming the child, there will be a dance of celebration with its own special music.

If a young woman has her ears pierced, the women do not miss this opportunity to celebrate in dance. They call in a musician and offer him a token payment, such as a package of cigarettes, for his services. He beats the drum, and they dance. The same thing happens when a woman decides to blacken her lips for beautification. In view of such practices, the Minianka men like to say that the women seek any pretext to dance.

Every Minianka village has a square where the village balafon is placed. This is the gathering place for all the village youth up to the age of twenty-five. The music played there is especially for the young and not considered appropriate for older people. Every generation has its time around the balafon and leaves it when of age to do so. The youth play this balafon and learn the songs and rhythms that go with it. Older people can go there only if invited by the young for special purposes such as showing them an old dance. This balafon of the young is played almost every evening. Only if the musicians are tired will there be an evening when the children and youth are not dancing around their balafon. It is music for entertainment, for fun.

Activities not involving music are rare in a Minianka village. Wherever they work, the Minianka dance and sing. Music softens a hard existence. It is present in daily life for work, births, deaths, marriages, and baptisms. Music is involved in the rituals of the secret societies and in the healing of mental illness. By itself, this music gets bored, so to speak. So it is always accompanied by its faithful companion, dance.

Dance

Dance, known as *hooro* in Minianka, like music, is not considered only an aesthetic expression. Taken by the sound of the music, the dancer enters into another level of reality, both communal and universal. In these circle dances, done in community celebrations, each individual has his or her rightful place. Not only the beautiful, the elegant, or sophisticated belong, but everyone. The dance possesses an invisible force that can draw a person farther than he or she imagines. When one is truly taken by the music, one becomes capable of movements that one could not have willingly done otherwise. Some people become so possessed by the dance that for several days afterwards they no longer have the same sense of reality as the average person.

We dance under many circumstances. First, there are the secular dances for everyone, danced for no special occasion, or at marriages, births, or the naming of a child. In celebrating together, we find no place for questions such as "What am I doing in this world?" or "Does life have a meaning?" It is like community preventive therapy. Life feels good. It is no small thing to dance in community. It is a great harmonizing measure.

Next come the initiatory dances performed expressly as rites of passage at various stages of a person's life. An initiatory dance, like the adolescent boys' circumcision dance with its special music, occurs only once for the individual. Of course it takes place with the coming of age of each set of boys, but only the initiates may dance it. We call this dance the round of the seasons. They learn it in the forest. The boys stand in a circle, holding long sticks. They tap the ground with the sticks and mark complex rhythms with sticks and feet. It is a strenuous dance, demanding strength and coordination.

Initiatory dances help the initiate to embody and express the mystery of the new status attained through the rite of passage. Some dances recur once a century. Many Minianka living today have only heard of them, as their time has not come on the ritual calendar.

There are dances for the dead during funerals and burials. If an old person has died after a full round of life on earth, these are times of grief and celebration. This and a fourth category of dance, the magico-religious dances performed by the great masters of initiation and the secret societies, are discussed in more detail in Chapter Eleven.

Since dances such as funerary dances are reserved for special occasions, they may not be practiced aside from when they are actually needed. And no one but a Komo initiate on a consecrated occasion may do the Komo dance. No one who has not killed a lion may perform the lion hunter's dance. Observation, concentration, and memory are needed to learn dances. They are seen and practiced only in the appropriate contexts.

The Bambara people of Mali have a dance called the *gomba*. Over a period of seven years the children learn this dance in secret, in the forest. It marks the passage to adult status. When their time comes to dance it in the village square, they are held to exacting standards of performance. If they sound a false note in the music or make a false step, they are supposed to die.

The Bambara have another dance that may not be practiced just for fun because it is considered sacred. It is presented as a theatrical ritual, showing a hunter in pursuit of an animal that embodies a spirit stronger than human beings. This dance is allowed only once or twice a year. It involves acrobatic leaps and twists that require complete concentration if they are not to be dangerous for the dancers.

In Minianka music, the dancer is a member of the orchestra

equal to the other musicians. The dancer's tempo is the same as that of the other members of the orchestra, and dancers sometimes even wear bells around their ankles. Like the other musicians, the dancer must move with coordination, discipline, and dignity. The dancer is not to show off but to communicate, following the training and rules of Minianka musicality. When the rhythm changes, so does the dance step. Dancing in disregard of the music is unknown in the tradition. Someone who repeats the same steps and gestures to different sorts of music is considered mentally disturbed, since this represents a breakdown of communication, awareness, and community.

If someone arrives at the village square disheartened and not wanting to dance, he or she will be encouraged to enter the circle in order to be renewed and to release the bad feelings. The dance restores the individual to wholeness and acceptance in the community. The Minianka say that the dance is the first occasion where two enemies can share something. Thus, in addition to being preventive medicine, dance is a factor of social reconciliation.

Stick Dances

We have a dance we call *dounouba*. It is for people who are threatening each other or are in an intense rivalry. After elders, family members, and friends have tried to counsel the disputants to no avail, the *dounouba* ceremony is held in the village square. The two men who are at odds each take a stick. The stick is round, about three quarters of an inch in diameter, and reaches from the ground to about the hip in length. The men face each other. The musicians play the drums with very exciting rhythms designed to bring out the stored-up aggressiveness in the feuding parties. The men engage in ritual combat, striking at each other and defending themselves with their sticks. In front of everyone else in the village, they settle their differences. The rest of the village will be left in peace, since not an ounce of their hostility remains unexpressed.

Some national dance troupes in West Africa have presented this dance in pantomime fashion to foreign audiences and called it the dance of the strong man. Originally though, it was not a spectacle, but a practical means of bringing real conflicts to a climax and to an end.

THE HEALING DRUM

Occupational Dances

Every evening there is music and dancing in the village square. When the musicians see a blacksmith go into the middle of the circle, they begin to play the blacksmith's rhythm. Because of my paternal Fulani heritage, they play the cattle herder's rhythm when I dance. If other ethnic groups are present, the musicians should know appropriate rhythms for them.

The dances derived from work are very old and represent the accumulation of centuries, even millennia, of human knowledge. Clever or stunning choreography cannot replace the significance of these work-based dances.

Daily life is so rich in movements, it is not necessary to invent special ones just for dance. The Minianka, like other African peoples, take these same movements and dance them in a celebratory manner. Each dance step has its accompanying music. The dances are not mixed together, just as one does not sow, hoe, and harvest all at the same time. In the evening, when the farmers gather around the village square after their day's work, and they dance the same gestures they had used that day at work, they affirm who they are in freedom, trancending the realm of necessity. Every musician in the village must know how to play the music of every profession. In following the dancers, the musicians show respect for the work the people do and provide the appropriate rhythms they need to express themselves.

The dance of sowing follows the actual gestures farmers use in planting seeds. If someone has never seen seed planted, learning the dance will be a bit complicated, and its movements may seem arbitrary. But the hand and foot movements are authentic. Knowing the life-sustaining significance of these movements adds to the value and meaning of the dance.

Dancers perform the hoeing dance bent forward, just as the farmers in their fields bend forward with the daba. The rhythm of this dance follows the actual work rhythm. Naturally, dance is not itself work. While the principal movements make allusion to work, the dancer is not restricted to only these movements. Many parts of the body move freely for relaxation and celebration.

The harvest dance imitates the way peasants cut the grain with their knives or scythes. Hunters' dances are hierarchically organized and reflect hunting methods: some set traps or spread nets, others shoot arrows with bows, some throw lances, others use rifles. The music also varies accordingly.

In the cattle herder's dance we see the movements and positions associated with his labors. He is often seen leaning on his herding stick, or standing like a bird on one leg with his free foot resting on the inside of his opposite knee. He holds his stick in one hand across his shoulders, and the other hand lies loose on the stick and dangles from the wrist.

It is pleasing to see someone who moves with the rhythm and doesn't fight against it or break it. This dancer is a friend of the music and makes the music visible. Spectators benefit from the harmonious feelings induced in them. It is not necessary for the dancer to force anything or to try what is beyond his or her capacity. Someone who does a small step well, who does not pretend to perceive all that the music contains, is appreciated for being true to his or her own reality. It is a matter of tactfulness toward oneself.

Dance of the Personality

In Minianka dancing, there is room for improvisation in what is called the dance of the personality. When a person comes to the center of the circle to dance, the musicians must follow the dancer. He or she keeps to the basic step but beyond that is free to improvise. The step guarantees that the rhythm is respected. The dancer will not change this suddenly or completely. Within the structure of the occupational dance, small gestures and refinements can bring out the individual personality. The dancer can take as long as necessary to feel satisfied. The whole night is available for dancing.

The musicians alternately relate the tempo of their playing to the circle and to the individuals who come to the center.* A person who weighs 300 pounds cannot be expected to dance at the same speed as one who weighs 100 pounds. A grandfather of sixty-five years will move differently from a youth of eighteen. The Minianka feel that a music of standardized speed does not take human differences into account and thereby fails to show adequate

---

*For music especially relevant to community circle dances, listen to "Were" on *The Healing Drum* audiocassette (see page 213 for ordering information).

respect for the individual. If a trembling elder enters the circle to do a dance he knows, the musicians honor him by following him. I have seen a very fat woman, much appreciated as a dancer in the village, get moving so that all her flesh took up the vibrations. It was a challenge to the musicians to follow her. One musician was inadequate—at least two soloists were needed, one to follow the movements of the upper body, another to follow the lower body. This pleases the onlookers as well, who may call out their appreciation of the combined skill of the dancer and musicians. Then when a small, quick dancer enters the circle, the musicians must respond accordingly.

Once I was playing drums in the village when a blacksmith entered the circle. We musicians sang out to welcome him. He started dancing slowly. It looked like he had drunk a bit too much. We followed him. He started moving back farther and farther until he was out of the circle. We couldn't see where he went. We played more and more strongly to bring him back into the circle. The music was intense. Still he did not appear. We didn't want to change the music until he completed his dance. Finally, a child went to see what had happened and reported back, "Hey, the blacksmith is asleep under a tree over there."

I once saw a ten-year-old child move to the center of the circle. He was dancing fast and stopped suddenly, pointed to his feet and challenged the musicians to follow him well. They became nervous. Their competence was being judged, and he exhausted the entire orchestra. Such circumstances are accepted and considered fair as long as the dancer is coherent and disciplined according to the basic steps and rhythmic structures.

The villagers look upon the touring African ballet companies as presenting tamed dances. The same steps of the original village dances are performed with choreography, and many things are changed in the process. This is not necessarily a bad thing, but it is not the best Africa has to offer.

The significance of the circle in Minianka community dances deserves to be appreciated. The circle expresses cultural values. The first value is continuity: no one can say where the circle begins or where it ends. All the people, young and old, are included in this continuum. The circle also expresses equality. All on the circumference are equidistant from the center, and all have a right to be in the center.

MUSIC, WORK, AND DANCE

When dances are performed on a stage, it can be a wonderful gift for the audience, but the meaning of the circle is lost in the process. In a circle dance even those who sit by the side and do not choose to join in the circle are involved in the dance. They can enter any time they want.

Trance

The Minianka say, "When there is dancing, it is not only the living who are present." The presence of spirits at dances is often signaled by the important phenomenon of trance. Trance occurs most often during the dances of the secret societies, which are discussed in Chapter Eleven. But the Minianka believe that the invisible world is also attracted to the popular dances held to express joy and to maintain good mental and physical health.

Trance occurs when spirits amuse themselves by playing nasty tricks on more susceptible people, those whose doubles flee readily.

The spirits mount these people's bodies and their doubles depart to another realm. The people do not appear to be in crises of hysteria or exhaustion. In the West there are dance sessions the goal of which is to lead people into trance. They dance for three, four, or five hours in a marathon session. This is supposed to provoke trances, but it may be the symptoms of exhaustion that are taken for trance in these cases. Certainly they are different from the experience of the Minianka, who are susceptible to the influence of sound and the invisible world, sometimes facilitated by ingested plants. These plants are not narcotics, like the commercial drugs with which many Westerners are familiar.

Trance phenomena among the Minianka are complex and not well understood. They are not amusements. Humans in trance are subjected to forces beyond their control. I saw a man jump into a well and leap back out as if propelled by springs. He was not just playing around with an abundance of energy—something beyond him was playing with his body.

Some Minianka in trance can be calmed through massage and the use of medicinal plants and brought back to normal consciousness. Their bodies may be trembling so much that they feel like shaking leaves under the hands of the people helping them. Little by little, their bodies relax, their senses contact the material world, and their reasoning returns. Meanwhile, the ceremony and music continue for others.

In the Minianka culture, as we have seen, dance is a medium for honoring work, for celebrating community, for affirming individuality, and for preventing mental illness. With the involvement of trance, dance becomes a way of communicating with the invisible world. This is an important function.

Dance is sometimes required as a remedial ritual when traditional laws are violated. When I burnt the sacred wood, a dance was required in addition to the sacrifice of the seven bulls, to pacify certain forces.

The power of dance and music are held in such esteem by the Minianka that the musicians learn special rhythms believed to calm lions, panthers, or other dangerous wild beasts. The musicians need to know how to play these rhythms correctly, without any wrong notes that would excite the animals and possibly endanger human life.

When the musicians play for the village dances, they seek first to be in harmony with the external, invisible world, to pacify the spirits that can be there in any corner. Prayer, washing, and wearing protective talismans are among the preparations for playing. If the spirits are excited, they will disturb the dance. Some musicians claim to see spirits among the people assembled for dancing. If they are good spirits drawn by good music, the ambiance can be agreeable. Bad music attracts bad spirits and makes an unpleasant atmosphere. This phenomenon exists not only in my native territory but around the world. The spirits in special locales respond to the traditional rhythms of the cultures established there. Knowing this, I contacted a Native American to learn about which rhythms were played around Montreal to contact and calm the local spirits. All over the planet—among Native Americans, pre-Christian Europeans, Tibetans—drumming has been used for similar purposes. It is important to draw on the local wisdom, to the extent that it has survived, in these matters.

The present population of North America does not sufficiently take into account the many ghosts and wandering spirits here. There have been many massacres and injustices that have never been dealt with ritually. The conquest of the native peoples and the slave system are just two examples. Too many people have died with hatred in their hearts and with their spirits never having been pacified. This is a disturbing influence.

In my view, as a Minianka, the present levels of violence are related to this, as is the popularity of music that excites the spirits. Coming from my background, I find the musicians here not conscious enough of the invisible effects of their music and of the need to exercise pacifying influences.

The Native Americans had dances to control fire and to bring rain. Among my people, we have dances to help a sterile woman become fertile. There is a biological aspect to this, but that is not the only level on which healing operates among us. Contact with the ancestors and spirits can also be helpful. We give an herbal remedy, along with a sacred word, and accompanying music and dance. Westerners may regard this as superstition, but they lose sight of the intention to restore harmony on all levels. They want to consider only material forces, but materialism cannot explain how dance and many other phenomena operate. Spiritual belief can be a powerful force also. For traditional Africans, perhaps eighty percent of our life is spiritually focused. Materialism is from our brains, spirituality from our hearts. When we dance, we do not explain why we put our feet down at a certain place. We dance. No long stories. We feel attracted to moving a certain way. We cannot analyze why some music makes us feel good. The responses of our hearts and bodies are personal and subjective. Nonetheless, I have tried to show the basic principles of dance for my people. This is not as self-evident or as universal as one might think: the underlying motivations for dance can be very different from one culture to another.

From the perspective of a traditional culture, it is surprising to meet people who are dancers by profession. They do not exist in our culture. In the village, everyone works, and everyone is capable of moving to music. This does not mean that we fail to appreciate people with special talent. I have seen such fine dancers in the villages that they could have been professionals here. At village dances, they are eagerly awaited by everyone else. When they finish their work, like everyone else, they come and dance. It makes people happy to see them dance; their talent enlivens the community.

We have no dance teachers, either. There are initiators, who teach a new group of initiates the steps of the dance appropriate to their ceremony. The initiators have their fields to cultivate just like everyone else. They cannot live from teaching dance alone.

In the village, our dancing shows whether we are in tune with our inner natures. Along with our music, our dancing helps keep us in tune with ourselves and in harmony with one another and the cosmos.

 10

SCHOOL

One day an old farmer with whom I had had frequent unpleasant encounters caught me and took me to the French school. This school was across the river in Zangasso, two and a half miles away, where my maternal grandparents lived. If I were enrolled in school, my father would have to find a more responsible herder, the farmer reasoned. Then his fields would less likely be trampled by my father's herds.

Originally I was not supposed to go to school, my sister was. The French administrators were arbitrarily enforcing schooling on the village. They had randomly selected a quota of the children, and my sister's name was on the school register, not mine. The farmer somehow negotiated with the administrators to keep me in school and send my sister home, and they accepted the exchange.

Mission Civilisatrice

Because colonial teachers tried to acculturate us to European values, the school made me and my schoolmates, in the eyes of our adults, almost lost souls to the community. This stigma further complicated my status in the village. I heard disparaging comments from adults concerning the influence of the French school on me. Eventually, I had to learn to integrate the two worlds, and it took me many, many years.

The French glorified their colonization of large parts of Africa as a "mission civilisatrice," a civilizing mission. They had not come to meet us as human beings with valid cultures of our own. Some people in France still asked whether we Africans even had souls. The colonizers were confident in the rightness of their mission to bring us Christianity and civilization.

Schooling was an essential arm of this cultural invasion. In the early 1950s, when I first attended school, about 250,000 pupils were enrolled in the colonial schools of all of French West Africa. While we pupils constituted only 1.5 percent of the total population of this extensive territory, the French hoped they could change our values enough to have an impact on our communities. They wanted to take us as far along in the Europeanization process as possible. Therefore, they started a secondary school for every twenty-five elementary schools, which was an unusually high number of secondary schools compared with what the British and Belgians established in their colonies.

Our parents were not considered fully human by the teachers in the French schools. The textbooks spoke of Africa rarely enough and then only referred pejoratively to the "natives," not to the human beings who lived on our continent. When the human body was discussed in biology texts, it was always pictured as being white with a tint of red, not brown or black. In their evangelizing, the teachers saw no place on earth for our "barbaric, pagan" beliefs and practices.

Our studies of history, geography, literature, and music were all centered on French culture. I knew Paris by heart and had to memorize passages about "our ancestors the Gauls." Africa was not studied. By implication, Africa offered nothing worthy of study. We were called subjects of a French overseas territory. Our goal was to become Frenchmen.

The French ideal was individual autonomy, and we children were encouraged to be independent from our parents. Our cultural value of obedience to our elders was condemned by the teachers as undesirable docility. They urged us to violate our sense of discretion, to speak about whatever we knew without regard for traditional cautions and prohibitions against revealing secrets. We were also encouraged by the French to feel ourselves the equals of our elders, to assert our knowledge and contradict them. This went against our village culture, wherein even someone who knew much would show good behavior by keeping silent.

Avocados

An example of this is a blunder I made that involved avocados. After several years of education, our French teachers began instructing us about the germination of seeds. They had us insert three toothpicks in an avocado seed. We would then place each seed in a glass of water with the toothpicks resting on the rim of the glass and the seed thus suspended halfway in the water. We listened to this lesson carefully. Our teachers explained to us the different stages of the sprouting of the avocado seed. We were instructed to observe what would happen to the seed after one day, three days, a week.

We were thirteen years old at this time. To the adults in the village, it seemed stupid to watch a seed in a glass. We did not even have glasses in our huts, since we used calabashes as our drinking vessels. My mother saw what I had brought home from school and assumed it was just a game that could not interest me more than a day. So she poured out the water and threw away the rest. Independently, all the other mothers did the same.

Back in school, our teachers asked us if we had observed the sprouting of the seeds. We said yes but could not give them any details of our observations. Finally, I admitted my mother had thrown out my specimen, and the other children joined in saying this had happened to theirs also. We still had to write out our texts, to be memorized by heart, about the transformations of the avocado seed, its changes of thickness, the number of leaves that came out, and so on. After all that, our teachers told us, the seeds were ready to be planted in the ground.

This lesson occurred in the month of May. In June, the rains started, and plants began to sprout. At this time, the elders planted avocado seeds. They held their ceremony and said prayers for the fertility of the soil. Then they dug a hole for each seed, dropped it in, and stomped the dirt over it.

I watched this, approached an elder and said, "Old man, that is not going to grow."

This experienced farmer was so surprised he did not understand what I had said. So I repeated myself.

He exclaimed, "What? You are telling me that? Look at that tree over there, and that one, and the other one. I planted those. Are you giving me advice? Before even your little mother came into this world, we were eating here."

He took me home and yelled at my mother and family about my improper upbringing. The elder pointed to his teeth and said, "Go tell your white people we have been eating well here without your advice."

At the end of the month of June, I had to write on germination for a test in school. I wrote that you say a prayer, dig a hole, drop in the seed, stomp dirt over it, and it grows. My grade was zero.

The position I was in was incomprehensible to both the villagers and my teachers. No one in the village could understand how I could presume to give advice to elders. The teachers who saw an examination answer such as I wrote could only conclude that we did not want progress.

When I was first enrolled in school, my father was happy with the turn of events. He took credit for having calculated it. Not considering me very intelligent, he was convinced I would last perhaps two days in school. He announced, "Yaya is a good-for-nothing. He even has difficulty living in our black society. Do you think he will be able to last at the white school there?"

His listeners proclaimed, "That's true."

He passed for a genius with this reasoning. At the time, the villagers did not want any of their children in school, but especially not the girls. They did not know what the white people were teaching in school and did not want to know. There was some confusion about the ultimate reasons for enforcing schooling on any of our children. In the past the French had enforced military service in the two world wars from which many of our young men never returned. There had also been enforced heavy labor. The specter of slavery still haunted our collective memories. The adults wanted to protect at least the girls from whatever misfortunes school might engender. There seemed no connection between the French schools and the future role of the girls as mothers and educators of their families in our traditional ways.

SCHOOL

My father bragged to other parents: "So, you have a child at school? I was able to get my daughter back out, and soon my son will be with me too." He was certain of my failure.

The elder, Nangape, however, told my mother, "You see, I said your son would go far. He is starting on his path now."

My mother humored him but believed more in what she was hearing in the village about it. She said, "That cannot last long."

Nangape held firmly to his vision, "You will see."

School was in session six days a week. I lived at my maternal grandmother's in Zangasso while I was in attendance and walked to Fienso to stay with my parents for Sundays and holidays.

The two days my father had predicted for me in school turned into two years. For the first year, from my point of view, I was going to school for the fights I could have before and after classes with the other boys. With a consistent record of zeros on my tests and assignments, I fulfilled my assigned role of village fool. I was last in my class.

Scholarship

One day, during the second year, my mother asked, "Is school difficult for you?"

"I don't know," I answered.

"What, you have been in school for over a year, and you don't know? How is that possible?"

I explained how school was for me. I got my daily spanking from the teacher. The dose was correct. My fights were exciting, and school had other advantages. I was comfortably seated, sheltered, and shaded. I no longer had to follow a smelly herd of cattle under the hot sun or in the driving rain. I did not even have to fear running into poisonous snakes. It was almost a vacation. All I had to do was sit there and listen to an imbecile who talked all the time and take the daily beating I was already accustomed to.

For committing the offense of speaking my native language, I often had to wear a dunce sign, the symbol of stupidity. This was a slate on which was drawn the head of a donkey. Supported by a string, the slate was worn around the neck like a large pendant. Only a stupid ass would speak the Minianka language, it implied. The other children would cry out and mock the one wearing the symbol. A couple of teachers would hold down the hands and legs of the offender while another teacher beat him unpityingly with a stick or whip. These beatings frequently caused blood to flow.

I got so used to wearing the symbol and being beaten, it did not bother me any more. The teachers, in turn, became so tired of beating me for speaking my language, they did not go to the trouble after a while. I profited from this situation and even saved some other children from having to wear the donkey head. I bargained, for example, to wear the symbol for a classmate in exchange for a few guavas. My stupidity became a valuable barter item for me. I traded it for fruit and saved my friends' skins in the same deal.

As far as I was concerned, things were going pretty well. Compared to what I had known before, it was a fairly tranquil life.

Finally, in December of that second year, my mother asked, "Is all that the other people say about you true? Are you really an idiot? You are proving them right. What about the predictions of Nangape? He is an old sage, a clairvoyant. We all respect that he has known much. Now I am starting to doubt his clairvoyance. In the past when he predicted something, it always came true. Everyone is doubting him because he foresees success for you."

I admitted to my mother I had never really made an effort in school. She urged that since I was there I might as well try. I was eager for this conversation to finish, and I promised I would.

Within three months, I went from last to first in my class. Apparently something had been registering in my mind after all during that period when I was taking it easy. Perhaps my fascination with music gave me some skill in picking up sounds even when I was not paying close attention. Now I found the sounds of the French language were clear to me. When I started to read, I quickly recognized the correspondence between the written symbols and the sounds, as if the program had been recorded in my mind.

The villagers could not believe I was the source of my own success. Since my mother was widely considered a sorceress, the answers to my examinations must have appeared magically. In spite of my being first in my class by that spring, when the average of my two years of studies was calculated, I had still failed. I was expelled from school. Then a new French academic inspector looked over the records of all the failures. He saw my long list of zeros followed by excellent results. He thought it made no sense to have expelled me.

SCHOOL

Meanwhile, I was herding cattle again. My father was content: "I knew he would be sent home. It was just a matter of time." Then one day a policeman came on a big motorcycle to look for me. Everyone stared as I was taken up on the back. I grinned, happy to have succeeded. I was driven back to school.

Whereas the other children in school were excused from any farming responsibilities, I was not. Since I had no older brothers, I still had to go out with the herds when not in class, to walk in the rain, to labor in the fields. My classmates with older brothers could relax in their free time, read comic books, play with one another, while I was in the fields with the other peasants. The popular opinion of me went unchanged.

The people spoke badly of my father as well: "Of the three brothers, he is the most stupid," they said.

This burnt away at my mother, ate into her heart. She said to me, "All I ask of you is that you grow up. May God grant you a long life. You don't have to be brilliant; just live. Remember, even if you are not a chief, perhaps one day a descendant of yours will become one. If you are not intelligent, perhaps your son will be."

The French educators had different ideas. They were preparing me for the nationwide competitive examinations for secondary school. My elementary school teacher was sure I would pass, and I felt the burden of living up to these expectations.

While walking to the examination, I passed a trader of the Hausa tribe who was selling all sorts of magical remedies. "Against the bites of serpents, I have the remedies," the salesman declared. "For you to be intelligent and successful, I have the magical charms," he promised.

I thought, "Ah, that is interesting." But I did not want my schoolmates who were walking along with me to know I was thinking of buying a magical remedy. While this was common practice, secretiveness about it was equally common. So I told them to go ahead. I would catch up later. I went behind the bushes and waited until my friends were out of sight. Then I ran to the tradesman and asked, "What was that you said?"

"I have something to make you intelligent," the man answered.

"Well, I am on my way to an examination," I admitted.

The Hausa clapped his hands and exclaimed, "Better yet!"

He went on to cite examples of students he had helped. The son of a certain man was now studying in France thanks to the remedy he had taken. "You don't even have to write the answers," the trader told me. "You just sign your name. After that, when you are ready, you place both of your hands on the paper. All of the answers will appear instantly with no errors."

I was delighted. I would not even have to think in order to pass the test. Such magical thinking was widespread in my milieu. My considerable anxieties were relieved. I purchased the charm and went self-confidently to the examination. The first part was the dictation. A French woman read a text in French. We students were to write down exactly what we heard. With five or more mistakes, we would be eliminated from candidacy. Previously, I had done perfect dictations. When the teacher began to read the dictation, I crossed my arms in front of me. Incredulous, she inquired, "Doesn't the dictation interest you, young man? You may leave if you do not want to take it, you know."

I assured her I was in fact interested. She went on to dictate the text. I continued to sit there, writing nothing. When the woman finished the dictation, I posed my hands on the paper, raised them and saw the sheet was still blank. As the teacher went through one last review reading of the text, I wrote furiously but was unable to put down the entire last five lines. This already amounted to more than five mistakes. I was automatically eliminated from the competition.

Once again I found my place with the herds. Once again, to my father's dismay, a new teacher arrived who saw promise in my record. Soon I was back in school. The following year I took the examination again and passed with the highest score in the Sudan. Naturally, the villagers dismissed this by saying the exam must have been easier that year.

I was sent to school in the city of Sikasso. This complicated my life. In the village mentality, the farther away you go, the more successful you are. Sikasso was nearby, about 100 kilometers southwest of Fienso. My score was of no interest in the village, only the distance.

Nangape

I entered a class of 104 students at Sikasso. Since the city was close enough to my village, I was able to come home during Christmas holidays. When the people saw me, they taunted me, "So? Is your schooling already finished?"

With the various aspersions cast on my worth, I had to develop a self-confidence to stand against all trials. People commented, "It is money, not merit, that sent Yaya to Sikasso." As always, Nangape, the elder, stood against this belittlement of my achievement. I learned to laugh when others denigrated me. Their words could not destroy me. When I started something in the village, and everyone said I could not possibly succeed, this encouraged me. I knew I would succeed.

Nangape helped me to learn not to trust what others said about me. I am not sure how he had originally read my character: he could have read in me directly, or divined through water, cowrie shells, or the stars. On all occasions, he expressed confidence in me and my potential. If others spoke badly of me, he barely paid any attention to it, he simply waved his hand in a quick gesture like shooing a fly. "Let them talk," he said. "They have nothing better to do. Keep walking along the good path. Don't listen to them."

One day, Nangape was supposed to play music in our family field to accompany the team of workers led by my mother. On that day, he showed his support of me, not through words, but through actions. It was during summer vacation from elementary school. My task was to bring out to the field a large calabash of water to quench the thirst of the workers. I carried it on my head. Along the way, I came across a classmate from the elementary school in Zangasso. He came from another village and did not know where the people of Fienso lived. He was supposed to find someone's home to run an errand. As we had no addresses in the village, I showed my friend to the house for which he was looking. Then I took up the water again to go out to the field. An uncle of mine, one of my father's younger brothers who had turned himself into my sworn enemy, had watched me guide the other boy and then return to my task. He came after me with a stick, grabbed me, unclothed me, and beat me with force. I delivered the calabash of water to fulfill my duty, but said nothing.

That day, Nangape ate and drank nothing while he was at our family field. He refused all offers. The beating delivered by my uncle was unjustified.

THE HEALING DRUM

Nangape said to me, "You will be grown up one day, and all of this will be ended. They will no longer be able to touch you."

He played all the hot day long but put nothing from our family home to his lips. His gesture spoke strongly. Everyone could feel his disapproval and the pain he felt on my behalf.

 11

RITUALS AND
CELEBRATIONS

Every Friday was divided for me between school and music. Beginning at four in the morning, musicians from many villages would come to play at my grandfather's compound. I awoke to this music and immediately went to be with the musicians, sitting totally absorbed and moved by the music until just before seven when I had to leave to be in class. At noon, I hurried from school to the village square, where the music continued. We had a three-hour break in the middle of the school day for lunch and a siesta. On Fridays, I was interested in neither. Music gave me my nourishment and repose. I had to run at top speed to be in class by three.

School never stopped me from participating in the social life of my community. In those years, not even one percent of us who went to the French elementary school succeeded in graduating from high school. It did not enter our young heads that we would be among the one percent. Just because we were going to school, our parents did not stop educating us in the ways of our traditional culture. In no way would they have entrusted the moral upbringing of their children to the hands of the white people. They did not even understand what school was supposed to be or produce.

THE HEALING DRUM

They had never seen any black people who were schoolteachers, engineers, company directors, or police chiefs. Sometimes parents came to school to ask permission for their children to be excused from classes in order to accompany their fathers in traditional ceremonies. By doing this, the parents hoped to spare their children punishment for absence.

Punishment took the form of beatings—so common in school that in one morning the teachers once went through twenty whips. One year I was designated to gather whips for the school director every morning before I came to school and to present them to him for their cruel use by our teachers. There was not a tree around the school that I had not climbed to break off branches. The bougainvilleas were being steadily denuded. All day long one heard the snap and crack of these woody whips from all the classrooms. Not a day passed when I was not hit from one to twenty times.

Occasionally the French school gave permission for a child to participate in village festivals. This was unusual, however, since the French only gave time off for Christmas and Easter. Those days meant nothing to us. Parents sometimes feared they would be imprisoned simply for asking to excuse their children from school. They did not dare to present their petitions as often as they would have liked.

When the drums were played at night, I was like all the other village children: I could not go to bed. The elders could not understand that we were supposed to go to sleep at nine o'clock to be rested for school the next morning. That was not their concern. Village celebrations were for everyone, young and old. Mothers danced at three in the morning with their infants securely fastened to their backs. Young children had never been excluded from community music and dancing. The elders did not see any reason why the French school, which took away some children for most of the day, should also force the children to be separated from the community at night.

For the six years during which I went to elementary school in Zangasso by day, many of my nights were devoted to music. I played the baforo drum then. My classmates danced. While the French colonialists tried to make their school our focus and main work, we enjoyed our nocturnal revels with our people. This was truly moonlighting.

130

RITUALS AND CELEBRATIONS

Even during school hours, if we heard the drums start playing for a ceremony in the village, we shut our notebooks and ran from school to the village square. Our teachers tried to put guards around the school at such moments to stop us, but the fear of being caught or beaten did not deter us.

Once a year the Maniah festival occurred in Zangasso. It started on a Thursday. We children waited anxiously at school for the first drums to sound. As soon as they did, we slammed our notebooks shut and fled. School was over for that week. The French people could do nothing about it. They had even built their school outside the village so we would have fewer distractions. The distance meant nothing to us. Those of us who were in classrooms bolted through the doorways and leapt through the windows. Those who sat in the shade of a tree for their lessons headed straight for the village. This was our holiday, and we claimed it.

Maniah Festival

The Maniah festival begins when the Maniah fetish is brought out of its hut. One rhythm accompanies the bringing out of the fetish, another its placement on the head of the person who will carry it, and a third goes with the procession, which takes the fetish three times around the village. The fetish is red. A conquered warrior customarily wore it. While the fetish was on him, it was believed a spirit could speak through him. If the person carrying the fetish were to let it fall, he would be condemned to death.

In the context of the secret societies, there are no messages that come from the invisible world to the visible one without passing through someone in a trance, or through someone who is considered mad. Initiations within the societies can qualify people to go into a trance as well as to prepare the musicians for their role in inducing trances and in bringing people back to normalcy.

For the Maniah ritual to be effective, a man and a woman must go into a trance state. Certain individuals are known to be susceptible to special drum rhythms played at the beginning of the ceremony. Assistants gather around these people in case they go into a trance. When a woman starts to tremble upon hearing the drums, she is held by other women, and her clothing is wrapped securely around her body. The likelihood is that this woman will be in a trance for the entire day, and she could easily lose her

131

clothing without being aware of it. This must be prevented. The Minianka maintain that it is not good for children to see their mother undressed.

This woman in trance then goes in front of the Maniah fetish. Only she is permitted this privilege. Everyone else must remain behind the fetish. The woman in trance enters into communication with the invisible world in order to chase away any evil spirits in the vicinity and to clear the passage for the Maniah fetish.

During one Maniah ceremony, I saw a man hit a tree repeatedly with his head. I have still not understood this. I saw another man in trance fall to the ground as if there were a hole there, but when I walked over the area, the surface was level without any holes. To try to restrain people in trance is not easy, for they are abnormally strong.

I saw my father in trance for an entire day during a Maniah ritual. His normal awareness and recognition of people were gone during that time. When he walked by me, I saw many wounds on his body. The worst part of it was that when he recovered, he could not remember how he had gotten the wounds. In a trance, people move suddenly and sharply. They may even run into walls, jump into wells. They become violent with themselves, lose control, and cease to behave in a human way. I once asked one of these people why he became so violent and ran into walls. He answered, "Every object I see looks like a beautiful young woman who says to me, 'Come and take me.' I try to reach her but I run into an object." That is all the man knows about it. Such people are considered to have departed from the everyday world to an invisible realm.

At night, during the Maniah festival, the orchestras take turns playing. This is called a musical conversation. The people talk with one another; they invoke the spirits and try to pacify them. They dance throughout the night. On the second night, only Maniah initiates may participate in the ceremonies that begin at midnight with the sounding of a small bell. On the last day of the festival, a Saturday, the fetish is carried back to its starting place and put away.

Komo Society

In the Komo society, there is also a trance medium. As soon as the music starts, he begins to dance and be transported in spirit. A man with a bell follows him. This is the interpreter, who knows the complicated language of the invisible world that comes through the mouth of the medium. Only certain initiates are capable of interpreting the spirit language. If the news is important, whether it is good or bad, the interpreter may stop the music to announce it.

I went with some friends to another village to hear the Komo music and see the dancing. Suddenly, the interpreter stopped the music. The message was that the Komo spirit had a job to ask of me. I myself did not understand the medium, but listened to the interpreter. He said I had come from a faraway village, which was true. If the people of my village did not make a certain sacrifice, a woman would fall from a tree. I was charged with bringing this message to the traditional chief of my village.

The traditional chief performs all the rituals and sacrifices related to the well-being of the community. All important messages pass through him, which he then circulates. He is the representative of the ancestors on earth; he maintains the customs and ensures the respect due to the elders. He is a man like any other, with his fields and his family. He enjoys no special privileges and exercises no power. He is in service to the community. He practices geomancy and is consulted every time someone wants to choose a new field to cultivate. In his turn, he consults the ancestors and nature.

The chief is descended from the first family that settled in a given village. The succession goes from father to son; there are no elections. The elders say, "Whether the chief is good or bad, it is necessary to unify around someone."

I fulfilled the task asked of me through the trance medium. I went to the traditional chief of my village, but the chief did not listen to me. Two days later, a woman fell from a tree and died.

Nia Ceremony

In the typical Nia ceremony, the fetish is transported from the village to the forest. Talking drums with bells are played, along with a sort of ten-string guitar and a metallic pipe with indentations, which is scraped with a stick. The music is played for two nights, beginning on a Thursday evening.

The Nia society is called secret, but these ceremonies are open to anyone. They have other, more profound activities that are only for initiates. The rhythms of Nia society music are especially aimed at promoting trance. I never play them at a show in North America. If someone were to go into a trance and start leaping about, others might think the person was having a psychotic episode. Even in the village, these rhythms are played only once a year. They are not for amusement.

The Nia music goes on all night, with some people falling into a trance. The spirits of Nia are said to choose certain people to be their messengers during the ceremonies. Anyone can be chosen. It is necessary to be on one's guard if one does not want to be a medium. The spirits speak through the most receptive people. The elders give trance-inducing herbs to those who want to enter this state more easily.

At times, a person may be given these herbs without knowing it. Some elders invite him to have a drink with them and drop the powdered plant into his calabash. As soon as he hears the music, his spirit leaves his body. The potential value of this is to enter into contact with spirits or ancestors and to become the medium for their messages.

I have seen people in trance jump into the middle of a fire, run through thornbush thickets, run into walls and break them. Some people lose control of their actions and need to be held for their safety, massaged, calmed, and brought back to consciousness. Upon returning to normal consciousness, the mediums do not remember what they said in their altered state. The music is intense until dawn, when there is a rest.

At noon, the music starts up again. The Nia fetish is taken out of the village to the square hut, where there will be a sacrificial offering. When the Nia fetish sack has arrived at its destination, a different musical rhythm is played to remove the spirits from those in trance and bring the people back to their normal selves. The celebrants line up in two rows facing each other and dance, with those who are in trance in the middle. It happens occasionally that someone in a row falls into a trance, and the dance continues until everyone is restored. There is no hurry. Sometimes the elders see that they need to make additional prayers. On the second night and day, the same scenario is repeated.

At the end of the ceremony, the musicians must deprogram any people still in trance to bring them back to humanity. This is called playing backward. At times, the music is stopped, because to continue could make the person ill. Massage and medicinal herbs also help to bring the entranced subject back to normal reality. Some people may remain in a trance for three days. No one can speak with them during this time.

The Nia celebration takes place in the month of April, when many Minianka festivals are often held. In the same month, the Nia celebration, the fire initiation, the funerals of the heads of families, and other rituals may take place. Funerals are significant community rituals among the Minianka, and we celebrate them in different ways.

Funerals

The Minianka say that a person lives to have a beautiful death. Someone who has lived well will be buried well. At the funeral, there will be tears over the loss, but death is not considered a catastrophe. When an old person has accomplished much in a full lifetime, his or her funeral is cause for celebration.

When we were young, every old person we saw represented a celebration for us. We thought, "There goes a celebration walking by; it's just a matter of days." We waited for the death so we could celebrate. It wasn't that we didn't want to see them any more, we just looked forward to the festival. When they died, we were bathed in tears. "Oh, we don't see him under that tree any more," we said to one another.

One old man in particular stands out in my mind. He was an elder of the community, a born educator without pity. He spanked us often. When we did something naughty, he chased us, and even if we tried to hide behind our mothers' skirts, he hit us. Then he would scold our mothers. Before making mischief, we would look all around to see if he was there.

When this old man died, all the children went to the burial at the cemetery. We helped carry him. We all dug the grave energetically. And what a celebration it was! All the orchestras of the village came and played. Usually, the ceremony of bringing the body from the village to the cemetery took six hours. For him, it took about ten hours. The burial was supposed to take place before sunrise, but by the time he was buried the sun was already there. Along the path to the cemetery, we stopped, we danced, we played.

Whenever I speak of the old people and our funeral customs, automatically this man comes to mind. I can never forget him. He left his mark on our whole generation. Everyone whose life had been touched by him came. Some of us came to honor him, others came because we felt free to make mischief without fear of spankings, others came for the celebration. Even the girls who had grown up and married husbands from other villages asked their husbands' permission to come to honor this old man who had educated them, spanked them, and given them much. It was very rare for one celebration to reunite everyone from the village like that. For three days and nights we were all together around the memory of one man.

While the death of an old person is a celebration, that of a young one is a great sadness. Initiation into adult status takes place at about the age of fourteen. Music will be played at the funeral of someone who dies before that age, but there will be no joy in it. It is painful to hear it and to play it. The people weep and cry out openly. It is especially heart-rending to see a mother lose her child. Even the death of someone under the age of fifty is considered premature and is felt painfully. Music is played to support the people in their pain. There are songs of mourning. Some women sing these well and come to sing on behalf of the most bereaved people. The community shares in grieving.

The funeral music itself varies according to the stage of the ceremony. Removal of the body from the home requires one specific rhythm. A different one goes with the washing of the body. Taking the body out of the family compound through the gate of the ancestors calls for yet another rhythm. The body is then carried to the place of the dead at the village square. The people dance around it there. It is the last time that the visible aspect of the human being, the body that has been left behind, will be seen. It lies wrapped in a white shroud. Special rhythms accompany this part of the ceremony.

On the way to the cemetery, at the first crossing of roads, the procession stops and plays more music. Upon arriving at the grave site in the cemetery, the people walk around the grave to a particular rhythm. Before lowering the corpse into the grave, there is still another rhythm, as there is when the corpse is placed in the grave, and the earth covers it. Then the farewell rhythm is played.

The musician must play all the music without making a mistake. He is trained for this, but he cannot practice these varied rhythms regularly. They may only be played if there has been a death. Once the musician has played the music, he commits it to memory through inner listening and visualization. The young musician usually finds funerary music very difficult to play technically and emotionally. When the musician's own father or other family members have died, he is not permitted to play at all.

As the people return to the village from the burial, no instruments are played. The women sing in choir, though, with hand-clapping and a bit of a dance step.

Throughout all the stages of the ritual of burial, the people are permitted to express their feelings through weeping, singing, crying out, and dancing. The musical support is much appreciated. When the corpse is laid at the place of the dead, ten orchestras may all be there playing in a small area. One is a group of talking drums, another of bells, and so on. The son of the deceased goes around to each of the musicians and gives them either some cowrie shells, clothes, or money. Often a funeral is very expensive for a family, and this can pose problems. To someone from outside the village, ten different orchestras playing all at once may sound very noisy. The villagers' ears become accustomed to it, though, as they walk around the square and tune in to one or the other group.

Having dwelt with a person in life, the Minianka also want to dwell with that same person at their death, to accompany the remains of the person all the way to the burial site. If I share in life with a friend, I can also help carry his body to the cemetery. I can also help shovel out his grave. Up to the last minute, I can live his death with him.

As death creates an imbalance in a family or a community, music can help restore balance. It facilitates the expression of feeling and makes the pain more tolerable. It acknowledges the loss but affirms that the community still lives and will not die.

Each death is ritually observed on two occasions, first at the burial and again during the dry season in a three-day celebration for each person who died during the preceding year.

The annual three-day funerals, called *bon-yi*, represent the collective pardon of the community. The deceased is pardoned for whatever wrongs he or she may have committed, and the living are pardoned for any transgressions against the deceased. The collective pardon of the community is believed to be essential for the soul of the dead person to be accepted among the ancestors.

The Minianka are not the only West African people with this custom. The Ibo also make two funeral observances. The first brings together the village. The second celebration assures the place of the deceased among the ancestors. Without this observance, the departed soul would be irritated and trouble the living. To die without being given a funeral is a sacrilege. For the old, to die well means to be buried with a great funeral, supported by music.

When the traditional chief dies, he is buried like any other elder, with the same ceremonies, the same music. During the dry season after a chief's death, however, there is a general funeral for everyone who died during the deceased chief's period of authority. The goal of this funeral is to cleanse the village. All crimes, fights, offenses to the spirits, insults to the ancestors, quibbling between husbands and wives, and frustrations between children and parents that occurred during this chief's reign must be settled in the three days before the naming of the future chief. No new chief should inherit any quarrels from his predecessor. If the successor proves ineffective, he cannot claim that the former chief left him the problems of a disorganized village—the village has been cleansed of crimes and natural imbalances.

For three days and three nights, the warriors' drums are played all around the village. In the daytime, the musicians go to the house of each widow whose husband has died during the preceding reign to separate his from his widow's spirit. The woman has been living in the village of her husband's ancestors. Since the husband has died, she needs to make peace with his ancestors and to be freed of any obligation toward them. (When a woman dies, a ceremony takes place to separate her spirit from her husband's spirit, but this does not occur during the time of general cleansing at the ritual chief's funeral.)

She bathes. Then she is placed in the middle of the drums. A deaf mute from another village performs the ceremonies. Through gestures, he interprets and communicates messages from the invisible world. He, the drummers, and the widow proceed to the crossroads. A red cock is sacrificed. The deceased husband's last remaining belongings are brought there so that the spirits can take them away and he will not come back to disturb the household.

The pact between the woman and her deceased husband's ancestors is considered ended with this ritual of separation. She is free to remain in her former husband's household or to move elsewhere, according to her own preference. If she chooses to remarry, any children who are born to her will be reincarnated ancestors from her present, not her former, husband's lineage. The husband's spirit is also free to be reborn through another marital union. Of course, because a chief may preside for many years, some widows go to their deaths without benefit of this ceremony.

The general funeral continues. The warriors' drums are played because they are provocative. It is necessary to bring out people's aggressiveness now, to incite them to insult one another. In the daytime, the people prepare disagreeable insults, the most atrociously spiteful words that could be said to anyone. The night is when they say them. As the drummers go around the village, the neighborhoods insult one another mutually. Someone might call out, "I thought you were ready to die, but you are cowards!" The insults and provocations are sung to the music and danced each of the three nights. This is group therapy on a village scale. Even married couples must say the truth to each other and enter the game. For the three days, it is necessary to think continually of offensive statements and to say them to the appropriate person. All other activities are stopped except for this. The violence must be entirely verbal, not physical. Resolution of conflicts is the goal. The drums are played well throughout the three days. A married couple who have experienced several of these cleansings in their lifetime benefit in their relationship. Children learn much from the process.

It is said that villagers who do not respect all the rules for this ritual of purification will die. No one is to keep in any grudges, harbor any resentments, plot any retaliation for the future.

After the three days, three small children, representing innocence, are each given a calabash to place in front of the future chief, who is the eldest male in the traditional lineage. The birthright of the eldest is held sacred. He is never skipped, regardless of his individual qualifications. Even if he is sickly, with hardly the strength to say yes, the council will work it out so that he has the last word, if only to affirm their decision. When a particularly incompetent chief happens to come into office, it is almost as if there were no chief, but things get done nonetheless.

The three warriors' drums that are played for the ceremony of village cleansing are also played when an adult male dies. Therefore, if they are sounded one day at noon, everyone in the village gets the message that a man has died. The drums cannot give his name, but people leave their work and assemble. The warriors' drums are also played at the ceremony of the sacred wood.

During the entire three nights of the village cleansing, the rhythm is never changed. There are no solos. The people cry out a lot, and this releases many tensions. Virtually the same song is sung throughout the ritual. Individuals improvise by adding their own rude remarks. Some people cannot even speak for a while after these three days, they have yelled so much.

The musicians are exhausted. They have maintained one rhythm relentlessly. At the beginning of the ritual, several musicians who know how to play the music come together. The three warriors' drums are placed on the ground in front of them. Then lots are drawn to see who will play the drums. The three chosen musicians must start at exactly the same moment, and finish at the same time on the same note. A drummer who fails to start with the others, it is said, will be taken by the spirits. The musicians must play for the entire length of the three nights of the ceremony. They are permitted to stop only when the drums are low in tone and need to be heated to tighten the drum heads. These are the same musicians who in the daytime perform the separation ceremony for the widow. The music for this ritual also is monotonous.

The new chief comes to preside over a thoroughly cleansed village. If a drowning then occurs, he cannot claim that his predecessor had disturbed the water spirits. Like the people themselves, all the spirits of the earth, trees, and water are held to have been pacified during the cleansing ceremony. The village is spiritually cleansed at the start of the new reign.

MUSIC AND
HEALING

During the year I attended school in Sikasso, I did not play any music, but the music was in my heart. I devoted my full outward attention to studying, yet my ability to recreate inwardly the traditional music of Fienso and Zangasso gave me a secret source of sustenance.

Sikasso, which is located on a wide plain, did not differ greatly from Fienso. The homes were mostly built in the same way: round mud huts and granaries with thatched roofs arranged in circular family compounds. But Sikasso is considerably bigger than Fienso. Today the city has over 26,000 inhabitants. Sikasso was an important city to the Senufo as it was the capital of a kingdom once presided over by King Babemba, who committed suicide in 1898 rather than submit to French domination.

When I went there, more than sixty years after the last resistance, the city still symbolized a will for self-determination. According to a Senufo saying, "We prefer to resemble our own grandfathers, not the grandfathers of others."

Each Sunday I went to the soccer game in the Sikasso stadium. I did not go to watch the match, but to listen to the balafon. I bought my ticket and boarded the big, open truck that went to the stadium. A balafon was played on the truck to attract people to the game. Like me, many among the throngs who attended went more for the music than for the sport.

I went to all the festivals in Sikasso. At night, I often went to the sites of local celebrations and danced to the balafons and drums. Whenever dignitaries from the government in Bamako came to give a speech, the local musicians turned out to welcome them with music. The politicians' words did not interest me, but the music drew me every time.

The Senufo music I heard in Sikasso is very close to the Minianka music of the villages of my childhood. The underlying base is the same, but the music varies because of different initiations and secret societies. The Poro society is important in Sikasso but does not exist among the Minianka. The Nia society cannot be found at Sikasso whereas it is well established in Minianka villages.

Since the Senufo live in close proximity to the Baoule tribe of the Ivory Coast, they have been influenced by Baoule rhythms. Similarly, the Minianka are closer geographically to the Bambara people of central Mali and have assimilated some Bambara musical tendencies.

A Life Threat

At Sikasso, I lived in the home of a former elementary school teacher. Scholarship money was paid to him for my room and board, which I shared with three other students. The family was complex. Through a series of incidents, my roommates and I found ourselves in a conflict with the teacher over our meals. When the time came for us to confront the teacher, his older brother who ran the household, and their wives about our dissatisfactions, I alone spoke up. My roommates stayed silent out of fear. Therefore, I was accused of wanting to disrupt the family.

Later, the teacher's brother called me to him and said he was going to kill me. No one would be able to find a trace of me left. He would use sorcery. The next morning, while everyone else was sleeping, he awoke, slaughtered a red cock on the terrace, and buried it. When the others found out, they said, "Yaya, you are dead."

While I slept, he had cut off a bit of my blanket and taken it as part of his ritual to destroy me. He also gathered the dirt where I had left a footprint. He was sure he could kill me like this. I confronted my would-be assassin. "It is too late," I told him. "Others, much more qualified than you, tried to kill me, but could not. You cannot touch me. I drank the milk from my mother's breast. You know I am Minianka. If you can kill me, then my mother is not Minianka. I challenge you to try."

Afterwards, he called me and said, "I have reflected and have pity on you. Otherwise, I would have killed you."

I declared, "I don't like that. Kill me. It is between you and me now. If you can't kill me, it means you are a bastard. Go ahead." He was old; I was young, thirteen years old. He became afraid of me and respected me. I knew where I was coming from. My protector, Nangape, was still alive in the village at that time. He could see what was happening from afar. I felt no one could harm me since I was under his protection.

Nangape and the Hernia

Something else happened to me at Sikasso. It strikes me as very comical when I remember it now, but it introduces the practice of healing.

Certain people are known as *djinambori*. This means that they possess spirits and can perform extraordinary things, for good or ill. I was walking to school and heard drums being played from a truck. This was to signal the announcement of one djinambori. This man claimed that in the wink of an eye he could make lions, snakes, and elephants appear. He would do this in the afternoon, along with other marvels. All day, I could think of nothing else but this promise and did not listen in class. I did not have the fifty francs required for admission, so I borrowed from several students, five francs at a time until I had enough. At that time, when an idea got into my head, nothing could stop me. At lunch, I managed to convince some more students to come see the cobras and lions with me.

After school, we walked in search of the show. We did not have the exact address but knew only the neighborhood in which the spectacle would be presented. An old man crossed our path. I asked him, "Do you know in which house the djinambori is going to make lions and other animals appear?"

THE HEALING DRUM

He answered, "Ever since I have been in this world, I have never heard of a man capable of making lions, snakes, or elephants appear out of the air. Are you asking me where God is found? I don't know where God's house is."

He went along. We were dissatisfied. No one could dissuade us from our quest for the man who could conjure lions. Finally, we heard drumming and found the house. We went in and sat down.

No one wanted to sit up front, just in case the lions that appeared might leap on someone. The showman played his drums and danced in front of us. Neither the drumming nor the dancing was very good. He took someone's scarf, poured sand over it, and threw it. Pieces of chewing gum came flying out. We gathered up the gum and thought that was good. After some tricks like that, the people started getting impatient. He showed us an empty basket, covered it, and then opened it to show that it was full of straw. That was fairly interesting. He played the drums some more.

Someone called out, "Where are the lions?"

He stopped playing and said, "Since you were born, did you ever hear your parents say they had seen someone capable of making lions appear? Or elephants? If not, then I am not the first man unable to do that. I do not know how to make lions, or even snakes. Don't expect to see that."

The people started to get angry.

He announced, "No one gets upset with me." He then took a calabash and said it was the devil's calabash. He put some water in it, raised it and looked to see if any water would leak through the holes in it. He spoke again: "Are you unhappy with me? I will do the following things to anyone who is unhappy with me. If you are a woman, you will be pregnant for the rest of your life. No one will be able to help you give birth, not even at the hospital. If you are a man, you will have a hernia that will fall all the way to the ground. I am the only person in the world who could treat you for it."

We sat there. Everyone tried to look happy. They smiled. He swung the calabash back and forth, and water came out of a single hole. He interpreted, "There is still one obstinate person in this crowd. Who is not happy?"

I thought, "I am the one." I knew myself, and I felt unhappy. He asked other people, "Are you happy?" They quickly responded, "Oh, yes, yes." He drummed some more and played gambling games. People kept losing money to him. A few angry spectators left. I imagined that maybe they were just tired and were going home to sleep. I knew for sure that I was not content. I stayed to the end. It was late.

Upon awakening the next morning, I was not able to get out of bed. In my mind, I was convinced that I had a hernia that dragged all the way down to my feet. I asked my schoolmates to help me. They asked why. I told them about my hernia. They saw no hernia. Four of them lifted me to carry me to the bathroom. I begged them to be careful of my hernia. They did not know what to do with me, but they laughed. My mind was turning. I would not be able to go to school any more, and only that man could treat me. The teacher from Zangasso knew what to do. He went to the high school and took up a collection of money. With the money, he sent someone to Fienso to bring my elder, Nangape, to me.

When Nangape arrived, I told him the magician had said only he could cure me.

Nangape came out with a proverb: "It is with one metal that you can cut another metal." He assured me the magician could not be so powerful. This gave me hope. Nangape began some incantations. I drifted off to sleep. He took a calabash of water and threw the water on me. I was startled awake.

He pointed and said, "You see, that is the water that was in your hernia. It is torn off now. Get up."

I started to walk around and found I had no hernia. While Nangape was there in Sikasso, he also settled the problem with the man who was going to kill me. It was not easy for a thirteen-year-old to leave the village and live in a town such as Sikasso without the protection of any elders. Some people took advantage of our beliefs and suggestibility. Nangape greatly reassured me.

Nangape was a master of the Minianka musical-healing tradition, and as such, he had a wide vision of life. To play and see as he did required continuous awareness of the atmosphere created by music, and of its impact on people.

The qualified musician penetrates into the invisible realms. While playing, the musician profoundly observes the invisible dimension of the dancer or listener to perceive whether this person is balanced or ill. To observe accurately, he must be emotionally detached from personal involvements and selfish interests. He must see into the invisible world while remaining fully conscious and clear-minded. If the music irritates the spirits and the invisible aspects of people, destruction ensues.

Sikiere-Folo

To see how the Minianka use music for traditional healing, the reader must understand how we conceive of illness. I cannot translate our expression *sikiere-folo* directly into a Western language without distorting its sense. When we say that someone is sikiere-folo, it means he or she is behaving bizarrely, unpredictably, not in a way our society expects, not as a human being should behave. Either the double has left, or the person is disturbed. We try to notice manifestations of strange behavior early, from small signs, so we can bring help before the condition becomes advanced and harder to treat.

To understand the Minianka conception of mental illness, it is helpful to look at how the individual fits into society from an early age. In the Minianka's extended families each child has access to many adults from a very early age; the child is not alone in the face of overpowering parental authority. Refuge can be sought with a wide number of relatives. Protection for a child can come from elders in the public square who look out for the interests of all the village. A child may also be under the protection of a secret society. A mother's age group can be approached as well. The age group tries to keep its members in balance. The children's age groups, for example, tend to minimize excesses and abuses and help keep their members in balance. In an age group each boy and girl can give free expression to any grievances or feelings about treatment at home. Social networking reduces the risk of isolation, and every child has some group in which he or she is taken seriously. Even a father who hates and rejects his child will be prevented by the society from acting out this ill will.

Naturally, the boundaries of permissible behavior by a parent toward a child are socially defined. A Minianka child may be beaten for misconduct. No one else on earth beat me as much as my mother, yet I do not hold her responsible for any problems I may have had later on in my life. Any spankings she gave me were deserved. I drove the elders of the village to the end of their wits. When I became angry, it was only my mother with her magic stick who could bring me back to reason. If she had not done this, I would be a failure today.

If I have one confidante in the world today, it is my mother. When I returned to Fienso in April of 1988, and most of the village danced till two in the morning, my mother and I sat together night after night in conversation. If I became angry about anything, she invited me to reflect on my feelings. As for my father, he never hit me.

When I look back on all I have experienced, I find no cause for any resentments against my parents. The focus of Western psychology on traumas suffered by children at the hands of their parents seems culturally alien to me.

Nonetheless, we assume no one is ever mentally disturbed without reason. This is our first principle in approaching illness: there is always a cause, whether from an invisible force, a person with hostile intentions, or from a biological imbalance. If the disorder is biological, we treat it with plants. If it is spiritual, we use music. Often we combine the two. They are complementary. We work on two levels, the visible and the invisible.

Our second principle is that whenever an individual becomes sikiere-folo in a society, the society itself is also disturbed. Two parties are ailing, the one recognized as a patient and the social group that has contributed to the loss of his or her senses.

Furthermore, a deranged individual may be a messenger through whom the ancestors or spirits give a message to the society. The invisible world has a big impact on our ability to keep our balance in walking a human path. Let us remember here that the invisible world is inhabited by Kle the Creator, by our ancestors, and by both friendly and hostile spirits.

The Hunter of Souls

One of our Minianka folktales warns about the ways of the bad spirits. The story is called "The Hunter of Souls."

Once upon a time, among the spirits, there were two hunters. As they left for the hunt one day, the first said to the second, "You say you are a hunter, but I have never seen you bring back any game."

"That is because I am a hunter of human souls," answered the second.

"Humans," exclaimed the first, "that is complicated. They are clever and nasty."

So the hunter of souls said he would show his friend how he went about his hunt, but first he wanted to know how animals are hunted.

"When you see a deer," said the hunter of animals, "you go upwind so it cannot catch your scent. You walk on tiptoes or crawl to approach silently."

Thus they hunted and ate what they caught. The hunter of souls was not content. He complained this was not enough. Once the food was eaten there was no further consequence. The animal hunter asked, "What is better about hunting the souls of people?" The hunter of souls promised to show him.

They went among a family. All was calm. There was solidarity among the people. "We cannot hunt here," said the hunter of souls.

They went to a second family. There was some noise, followed by insults. Then it calmed down again as the people made peace and joked. "We cannot hunt here either," observed the hunter of souls.

In the third family, there was a great tumult of insults. The tensions persisted. "Here we can hunt," spoke the hunter of souls. "You take possession of that one over there. I'll take possession of this one. They will fight and nearly kill each other. We don't have to defeat them. They will do the work for us." The fight occurred as predicted. "That is how we hunt," said the hunter of souls. "We look for where the people are divided by conflicts."

The two spirits set about their work, adding to human misery in many families.

Finally, the spirit who had hunted animals asked, "What good is it to disperse humans and turn them against one another?"

"Can't you see?" asked the hunter of souls. "When the humans are united, they are stronger than we are. That is their strength. To disperse them is the best of things for us. When they fight against one another, they leave us alone."

One evening, these two spirit hunters came to a village where all the people were dancing in a circle, making music, enjoying themselves. The humans were not vulnerable to the spirits.

"We can't find a mount to ride yet," said the experienced hunter of souls. "But wait, you will see."

They waited a few minutes until the people started to break up. It was then that they could possess them, drive them out of their minds, provoke discord and divorce.

The implication of this folktale is clear. Harmony among humans is the best protection against bad spirits. Similarly, the misery of becoming sikiere-folo, even if it involves nonhuman elements from the invisible world, can still be traced back at least in part to human conflict.

The individual human being stands exposed and vulnerable to malefic forces that can come from other people as well as the spirits. These forces affect that aspect of inner human nature known to the Minianka as the double.

Illness

A person's mental balance may be destabilized by disappointment in life, such as that suffered when a beloved partner leaves, never to return. Someone else might have wanted to pursue certain studies, failed to do so, and consequently become embittered. There are many ways in which people become disturbed when their expectations and hopes are not met.

If the disappointment has been too severe, it can become an obsession that is very difficult to treat. A man in Fienso once fell in love with a wife of one of my uncles. Since the man could not marry the woman, he became crazed and inconsolable. For a treatment of disappointment to be successful, some compensatory element must be found. This man's attention was redirected to a more appropriate woman.

Physiological problems may also affect psychological equilibrium, as in a physical trauma such as a blow to the head. There is also a category of mental disturbance that comes from genetic deficiency. The Minianka call this type of disorder one that came through the milk, referring to the earliest nursling stage. These we cannot treat.

People in the village who are selected by the ancestors or some spirit to bear messages from the invisible world are successfully treated for the loss of self-possession. However, the designation of former fool remains with them for the rest of their lives.

Another kind of madness can be brought on through failure to fulfill an obligation toward the invisible world. This is determined by the practitioner the family invites to take responsibility for the case. He may use divination or learn through someone else who goes into a trance and communicates a message from the ancestors or spirits. Such madness can be caused by offenses against the ancestors or spirits.

Frustration, such as that from sexual impotence, is treated by the Minianka with herbal remedies, along with the important ingredient of inspiring hope in the afflicted individual.

Whatever the case of imbalance may be, the villagers do not reject the individual or say that he or she alone has a problem. The community has a problem. Any one of its members is affected by the whole and, in turn, affects the whole. A Minianka proverb states, "If you are out walking and see a scavenger feeding off the corpse of a human being, do not say, 'Scavenger, leave the flesh of my fellow human in peace.' Rather say, 'Leave my flesh in peace.' " Humans living in community cannot rightfully step outside the circle of concern for the misfortunes of our fellow humans. Neither should anyone say, "Our society is corrupt, but it is not my problem."

Diagnosis

While playing for community dancing, the Minianka musicians may sense disturbances as they manifest in people's dancing. When they amuse themselves, people reveal their serious side. As they relax, they let out their suppressed tendencies. The fact that each profession has its characteristic dance steps and movements gives valuable diagnostic indications of a person's inner balance. When a blacksmith comes to the center of the circle, the musicians play the smith's rhythm. If he dances like a fisherman, the musicians know right away that something is unbalanced with him. It is said that he is possessed by a fisherman spirit, as the spirits, like humans, have their occupational specializations. If another person rolls around no matter what kind of music is played, the nature of the spirit that has possessed him is revealed. Each spirit provokes characteristic movements, and these are described in folktales that the elders repeat. These tales convey insights and give information acquired by the ancestors.

The domain of sikiere-folo is vast. Some disturbances do not wait for music to come out. For example, someone goes into the bush and suddenly becomes haunted by a spirit that cries out after him. He may take off all his clothes. According to a traditional saying, "You can hide your fool at home until the moment he walks down the street naked." Or, people suddenly explode in a rage with no warning signs. There is no time to investigate when they were first afflicted by madness, so revealing a problem through music is no panacea.

Village musicians never advertise as healers. When we are playing and notice a dancer behaving abnormally, we keep silent about it at first and continue to observe. If we still sense the person is disturbed, we discreetly approach the family to inform them of what we have seen. We ask them if they have noticed anything unusual and if they are aware of any conflicts in the individual's life. We extend our inquiries to others, such as members of the age group, if our first suspicions seem to be confirmed. We report to the family on what we have learned.

It is up to the family to recognize that one of their members is becoming sikiere-folo. They will then ask a musician of their choice to assist them. Through their own observations and word-of-mouth, the family determines which musician can help with the healing. The relatives will approach the musician and say, "We have this kind of problem in our family. We know you are effective with certain herbs. We believe you can be the one to help us."

In some cases the person is harmless, the disorder mild, and only a little needs to be done. An example frequently seen in Africa is people who are attracted to filth and garbage. They like to pick through the rubbish. They may prefer to make their home next to the dump. These people are looked upon as most likely suffering from a disappointment. In looking through the garbage heap, they seem to be searching unconsciously for what they feel they have lost or for what they have never achieved. We say they have been possessed by a rummaging spirit.

The community can come to their aid. First of all, we do not become indignant when we see them picking through rubbish. We do not call them names or throw stones at them to drive them away. Meanwhile, the family seeks out the musician who can help, and the treatment starts. We do not become ashamed of such people and hide them away from public view, nor do we deny the problem. We allow the person to act out this behavior, which harms no one, until effective treatments and rituals bring about healing.

Another category of disturbed people take themselves to be particular animals. Still others think they are seeds or plants. Some crawl on the ground while imagining they are snakes. If you go to Africa, you will see this behavior.

Discussions with the family at their compound help the musicians to verify that disturbed behavior and thinking are manifesting in daily life, and confirm the diagnosis made at the community dance. It was not just a temporary trance or possession. Family members, friends, and elders are consulted in order for the healer to find the right approach to healing. At times, the ill person is sent away from the village. Removing the disturbed individual from the disturbed social environment that led to the illness can be a powerful therapeutic measure. At other times, herbs are gathered to treat the symptoms. Appropriate musical remedies may be applied.

By talking with the family the healing practitioner also treats the individual's social environment. If necessary, a family council or a village council is called. Everyone with anything to say voices his or her views. Rituals for bringing peace to the community may be needed. Dialogue itself, for as long as necessary, in the family compound or in the village square, is the main way of bringing change to the social group in relation to a disturbed individual.

Everyone is reminded that the goal is for the person who has been sick to be reintegrated as a normal human being into the group. The practitioner may insist that people exercise self-restraint and treat the person as normal without making derogatory, insulting comments that provoke disturbance. Vigilance with our own behavior can be hard on many members of the community, yet we understand that it is often necessary and try our best to restore our harmony.

The inquiry to discover the cause of sikiere-folo often continues over a period of time. At some moments the disturbed person is probably more lucid than at others. The patient sometimes lives in the musician's home for the entire duration of the treatment. This gives the healer ample opportunity to observe. Often several patients are there at a time. Very violent ones need to be tied for their own and others' safety.

It is difficult to treat severe cases of disappointment in life, when people lose their hope, self-respect, and reason for living. One can sustain the loss of a mother, father, or spouse, but once hope and motivation are gone, it is difficult to carry on with life. An external loss may precipitate the internal loss of will. For example, a woman is respected in a household where she has her role and place. Suddenly she is repudiated by her husband. She goes through a number of dissatisfactory relationships while progressively losing her self-confidence. Finally, she is recognized as sikiere-folo. She awakens from sleep each morning with no positive aspiration for herself or anyone else. The healer must work, whether with herbs, music, or words, to restore trust and hope in such a case.

The village musician also needs to know the symptomatology of certain parasitical infestations that cause psychological symptoms. Correctly recognized, they can be treated with the appropriate plants. Filariasis causes disturbances of the optical system, so that affected people think they are seeing worms, snakes, or monsters. If unrecognized and untreated, this condition could cause real mental imbalance.

Epilepsy is another condition that may be confused with trance possession. The sound of a bell being rhythmically played and the flickering light of the fire can set off an epileptic fit. Villagers with this condition are counseled to avoid such irritants to their vulnerable nervous systems. They will be warned against some types of music and looking at fire. Traditional methods may not cure them, but the frequency of their crises can be reduced.

Dreams, Divination, and Spirits

The diagnoses of the Minianka musician-healers combine analytical with intuitive skills. I had a friend who played the talking drum and could foretell the time of death of fellow villagers. People avoided him. Even though he spoke of what was true, most people preferred not to know. Once I was with him when he fell asleep for about three minutes. During the sleep, he said, he saw some images like a little nightmare. When he awoke, he spoke the name of a man who it turned out had just died. Another time, I was going to invite an orchestra to come to the village to join in a celebration. He told me not to do it because a death had occurred that would prevent the celebration. He told me not to question him further, but to be happy that it was not my body in need of burial. Through other dreams this man, who was not old, learned how to treat certain illnesses. He did not know how he did this. He had never been taught by anyone else. It was a gift of his.

While growing up in Fienso, I always knew that dreams were an important source of learning and that some people learned much through them. Our healers are often guided in the use of plants through their dreams. Naturally, one needs to know how to interpret dreams. If one dreams of falling from the Eiffel Tower, this is not something to experiment with in waking life.

In my own life, music has come to me in dreams since my boyhood. Often I dream I am playing in a traditional Minianka orchestra. When I awake from sleep, I try to remember the rhythms I was playing in the dream. My practice of music has been much enriched in this way.

Varied means of divination are also practiced in Minianka culture. Some practitioners with the necessary talent and interest see images that reveal to them the nature of the problems. Others use a mirror. In such ways they might divine that there is a quarrel and someone has fallen sick because of the ill will of an adversary. Or they see that someone has neglected the funeral rites of a parent or obligations toward a secret society. Divination can be helpful when the disturbed person is traumatized and not able to answer questions.

In the case of a disturbed person who is possessed by a spirit, the diviner determines what spirit it is. Each spirit has preferred instruments, songs, colors of clothes, plants, and sacrificial animals. After diagnosis, the sick person is dressed in the clothes of the designated color, and the indicated music is played on the appropriate instruments. The intention is to transfer the spirit to the sacrificial animal. The patient may spend the night in proximity to this animal. On the following day, the sacrifice will take place. It might be a red rooster or a white ram with a black collar. The ritual must happen at a designated time that depends on the spirit in question. As part of the ritual, the patient may have to learn the spirit's dance, even if it is outside the patient's profession. After the exorcism has been completed, the patient may receive a talisman for continued protection. It is worn on the body and contains something from the sacrificed animal. An annual ceremony involving another sacrifice reinforces the pact with the spirit so that the person will no longer be bothered.

When I came to Montreal, I experienced a disruption in my life caused by a water spirit; it was an occurrence to be expected and dealt with properly. By my birth, I have an affinity with the element of water. Montreal, where I now practice my music, is an island and so surrounded by water. Spirits are attracted by percussion. As I am not a native of North America, I do not know the rhythms the Native Americans used to pacify the spirits of this place. So for three years in Canada I was disturbed. I did not despair, but my behavior was intolerable to society. People thought I was suffering from culture shock. Walking along the streets, I would yell at people and criticize them for no apparent reason. It was a very difficult time for me.

I even sought out some Native Americans to ask if they knew of traditions concerning the problem I was facing with respect to the spirits of the place. The Native Americans I approached respected my question but did not have the necessary knowledge to answer me. When I visited Mali in April of 1988 I was treated for protection from it. The treatment involved a plant that grows along river banks, the wearing of white clothes, and other measures.

Disturbance by Ancestors

In the Minianka culture someone who was temporarily disturbed because he was elected by the ancestors to transmit a message to the community has no reason to feel ashamed. To the contrary, it is an honor, although normal life is disrupted for a while.

I remember from my childhood a man in Fienso who had never married and spoke insultingly to the women. He would cry out vulgarly in a manner that sent the women running away from him. His insolence was unprecedented. I asked my mother, who was head of the secret society that defended women's interests, why the man was tolerated. She answered that he was giving lessons through his bizarre behavior.

During that time in the village, many of the traditional customs regarding relations between the two sexes were being neglected. Minianka women are held especially responsible for maintaining the unity of the community. This man's often obscene outcries served as reminders of the moral code with respect to marriage and much else. He was deranged; yet the effect on the village was to reduce the abuse of customs. He was seen as an ancestor, come back expressly to remind people of the path they were straying from.

Restoring Health

Once a person is healed of a psychological disturbance, reintegration into the daily life of the village needs to be accomplished. The age group plays an important role in this and helps the individual return to working and participating in the community dances with everyone else. This is the first step taken back into society. The age group members address the person as "former fool" to see if he or she reacts strongly. If so, the term will be applied until the person can accept it calmly for the simple fact that it is. Thus the age group helps the healed person avoid denial. Accepting the role of former fool makes one immune to derogatory remarks about the past.

My own age group assisted me when I returned to Mali in 1982. I had already passed through my dark period in Montreal. Back in the village, people repeated stories they had heard about me, that I was dead or crazy. The wounding things said about me in my earlier years with my age group made me immune to all sorts of insults. One by one, the members of my age group came to see me. When they realized I was well, they said, "We are so happy to see you, and to find you normal. When we heard upsetting things about you, we felt as if we were all affected."

While the age group cohorts help to inure the healed person to insult, others in the community must respect him and refrain from making injurious comments. The age group is the man or woman's staunchest defender, encouraging him or her to dance in the evening, to work in the day. There could be forty members of the age group, and their support can be strongly therapeutic.

Beings of the Bush

Spirits are also known as beings of the bush. The Minianka have a tale that explains why humans cannot see them.

Once upon a time, there was no distinction between the visible and invisible worlds. Humans and the beings of the bush were neighbors, yet they kept their distance from one another. They talked the same language. The ancestors who had died could come back and be seen. Even Kle, the Creator God, could appear. All the discord that has ever since divided the two worlds began because of the following incident.

In a village was a youth who wanted to leave the community. He did not want to have anything to do with it. There was too much jealousy and pettiness. He thought that in the bush he could cultivate his fields without being bothered by the faults of his fellows, and so he went there.

A being of the bush saw him. He had never seen a human so close before, and he admired his short hair. The hair of the being of the bush reached all the way down to his heels. It was especially hard for the being of the bush to walk through the woods as his hair would get tangled in the branches. While he recognized that humans had many weaknesses, just as the beings of the bush did, he appreciated that with short hair, the humans could at least enjoy more freedom of movement. So he asked the youth to cut his hair for him. The young human obliged and cut it off completely. The bush being felt happy.

Everything was fine until he went to a stream for a drink of water. He bent down to drink and saw his own reflection in the stream. Oh, how monstrous he looked! He had never seen such a sight before. How could he return to his community and be accepted? He tried, but as soon as he approached his family, they all fled. Finally, when they identified him, they punished him. He no longer looked like he belonged to them, they said, he had become like a man.

The beings of the bush had a council and decided to send the short-haired spirit back to the human who had cut his hair to demand that the hair be put back. The spirit returned to the youth who had left his village. On hearing the demand, the youth was perplexed. He did not know how to put back hair once it was cut. Even though he had rejected his community, he had to return to it to get advice on how to do this.

After three days of reflection, the village council gave the youth a strategy. He went back to his fields and told the being of the bush that he would put back the hair if the being could remove all traces of its footprints and handprints on the youth's fields. So the bush being, not knowing how to accomplish this task, went back to its village. There the conclusion was evident; the humans wanted a fight with the beings of the bush. The two would wrestle, and there would be a referee. If a human could put a being of the bush down on the ground or vice versa, the loser would be slaughtered.

The contest was well attended. All came, including spirits, ancestors, and the Creator, Kle himself. A crow was chosen as musician to play the balafon. Because the consequences of losing were to be severe, the two sides reconsidered. They made a new pact and decided to ask Kle for his judgment. If they wrestled and the loser were killed, enemies would be made.

Kle asked the youth what he wanted to become. He answered that he wanted to resemble his father. Kle put the human in the right, because he had done nothing to provoke the trouble. Kle made the beings of the bush invisible so the conflicts between them and the humans would cease. They would inhabit different realms. However, some of the beings of the bush were embittered by the decision. Since that day, whenever they see a human with weaknesses, they mount him and haunt him. Whenever a human wishes harm on one of his fellows, the evil spirits are ready to serve a harmful purpose. They work in alliance with humans who are malevolently disposed.

The ongoing difficulties people have with spirits stem from an ancient rivalry. Humans have the favored position in the cosmos. The beings of the bush are wild. They envy humans, yet wildness and human culture are irreconcilable. Thus, the bush being wanted his hair back, that is, his wildness restored. The youth who went out into the bush alone to cultivate his field must return to his community for help. He could not be just solitary and wild. He realizes this in the end, when he tells the Creator he wants to resemble his father. He can return the hair to the head of the bush being only if the bush being can remove all traces of its presence from the field. The bush being cannot do this either. Symbolically, although humans live through culture, including agriculture, they cannot live without seeing some traces of wildness in their fields, that is, in their own cultivated natures.

There is something in nature still that envies humans their favored position with the Creator who judged in their favor. The folktale points to a primordial conflict that makes humans vulnerable to invisible forces to which they are akin, but from which they are always separate. Even the Creator's judgment could not efface envy and conflict from the earth.

Human madness—going wild—refers us back to these primal problems.

The breakdown of harmony in the human community is the precursor of any conflict between humans and spirits. It can lead to possession. Harmony and solidarity among humans is the best protection from that form of mental disturbance recognized in the culture as spirit possession.

When humans are dominated by their weaknesses, such as envy, jealousy, greed, hatred, or ill will, there is a breakdown on two levels. By definition, community has broken down, since it depends on mutual support. Moreover, individuals break down. They become prone to losing their souls to wild forces that possess them. They no longer behave as humans, by human values, with reason, love, hope, and other virtues. They are seen as mad, foolish, insane, or possessed. Human intervention, that is, the restoration of community, is needed for the restoration of the individual.

Music and Healing

Having surveyed various aspects of Minianka views on psychological disturbances, we are now ready to examine more specifically how music is used as a healing power. If a musician has been engaged by a family, and if the appropriate observations, interviews, and divination have determined that the disturbed individual is possessed by a spirit, a healing ritual that involves music is held in the village square. Concerned family members, age group members, and healers join in the circle, preparing to dance around the person being exorcised. The first music played by the musicians is intended to calm the people and spirits in the neighborhood and throughout the village. When the musicians feel they have accomplished this goal, they bring the person to be treated to the center of the village square.

Possibly the person slept the night before next to a sheep that is to be sacrificed as part of the ritual. Possibly another animal will be slaughtered. Each ceremony varies according to what the musician in charge determines will be effective. At this stage of the ritual, the musicians play the rhythms known to be appropriate for the spirit that has been identified as possessing the patient. For example, some spirits respond to the blacksmith's rhythm. The patient may not be a blacksmith himself, but he must learn the blacksmith's dance. Performing it helps free him of the spirit. Once he has been healed, he still dances to these rhythms periodically at times of initiations, ceremonies, and sacrifices. The dance and rhythms help keep him free of spirit possession.

The most effective music for collective healings, such as funerals and clearing the sacred wood, and for healing individuals uses monotony. Once the musician responsible for the healing finds a rhythm that suits the patient and causes no fright, he continues it. This goes for the drum tones themselves. The traditional drum produces three tones: low, middle, and high. A patient whose illness is caused by a trauma may be enervated by the low bass tone, so it should be avoided in this case. The hysterical patient may be more agitated by the high slap tones.

Once the right sounds are found, the rhythm is not changed. The musician plays for as long as necessary, perhaps three hours, the calming, stabilizing rhythm and proper sound combination that help restore the disturbed individual to inner balance. It serves no purpose for the musician to vary the music. In fact, if the music changes, the patient will not change. Through the monotony of the music, joy returns.

When a group of musicians circumambulate the village several times for a collective healing ritual, they do not vary the rhythm. They abstain from improvising, not from lack of imagination, knowledge, or talent, but to serve a therapeutic purpose. The Minianka use of musical monotony is similar to such well-known practices as autosuggestion, affirmations, and mantra recitation. Each of these is held to be effective only through repetition.

The Minianka musician who heals does not necessarily fall back on a repertory of established rhythms. Determining the right music in each case is a highly individual matter. No predetermined formulas are given. He needs to create a dialogue between the sounds he produces and the responses of the person he is treating. Through his trained observation, he discovers the right rhythm for his patient. It may be a new rhythm, uniquely indicated for the case before him.

Agitated rhythms may be used if the patient needs more movement. They provoke the disturbed person to expend excess energy. Often strong methods are used. Some Minianka healers go so far as to give blows with a stick to enhance the provocation in such cases. Their intention is not punitive or sadistic but therapeutic. They are bringing out the symptoms of the disturbance, stimulating a release of energy. Otherwise the patient is likely to wake up in the night and scream out because of the build-up of blocked emotional energy. Once the catharsis is triggered, the musician continues to stimulate it until the patient is pacified. Then the appropriate, monotonous rhythm is played. The calming, continuous quality of the music supports the healing process.

How music can facilitate psychological therapy is perhaps ultimately a mystery. Since psychologically disturbed individuals are rhythmically disturbed as well, the use of the healing drum for sustained periods of time at a steady rhythm that suits the patient is a potent remedy for body-mind healing.[*] Through the ears, the entire nervous system is affected. Sound energy is transformed into bioelectric nervous energy. As the brain waves and rhythms of internal organs are stabilized, the person functions as a more synchronous whole. What is healing if not making whole?

Finding the suitable rhythm is the most difficult skill for the healer musician to learn. The same madness with the same symptoms in two people may yet call for different individualized rhythms. One factor the musician takes into account is the temperament of the patient. Is it a lethargic individual or a high-strung, nervous one? Temperament greatly influences reactions to music.

The musician can find the right rhythm only through attuning himself to the patient's deepest inner need. And only through staying attuned throughout the playing can he play the music effectively. If the musician becomes disinterested and mechanical in playing, the music is altered. The musician himself is an integral part of the therapy. There can be no remedy in the music without the musician's committed involvement.

European and Western-educated Africans have at times attempted to mix African with Western medicine. This has been the case at an institute for African psychiatry in Dakar and at the so-called hospital-villages of Zaire. They have sought to learn the healers' practices as if they were formulas: they collected herbal recipes in combination with the playing of drums, sacrifices, the recitation of magical words. They were disappointed when their experiments did not work. A vital ingredient was missing: belief.

---

[*]For healing music played on the water drum, listen to "Dji-Dounou" on *The Healing Drum* audiocassette (see page 213 for ordering information).

THE HEALING DRUM

Western science is based on an attitude of objectivity, neutrality. African medicine requires the involvement of the healer in the community and its faith.

From the perspective of modern Western culture, the close association of music with healing in Minianka culture may seem an improbable combination. Although there are music and dance therapists in the West, the domains of music and medicine are widely viewed as separate. What has been forgotten in the West and, fortunately, is being rediscovered, is that music itself is a remedy. It gives joy. Even someone in good health can be lifted to a higher level of health through music. It can calm or stimulate according to the needs of the people and the occasion.

The Musician-Healer

In the tribal culture, playing an instrument may be a basis for working as a healer. Traditional music embodies much knowledge. The musician knows how to give therapy, to bring joy, to console during the most difficult moments of grief, to be disciplined and serious during rituals. This requires a mature being in all respects.

In his maturity, the musician must not be impressionable. He needs to stay calm and centered regardless of what is going on around him. For example, in the fire ceremony, a dancer may put fire in his mouth. The musician would not be able to play if he were shaken by paranormal events such as these. That in turn would result in an interruption of the musical support to the dancers' concentration and could have negative and dangerous repercussions, such as the dancers' being burned.

Another aspect of the musician's essential knowledge is self-protection from negative sorcery and evil spirits. Music facilitates communication between the two worlds, and he needs to protect himself from the invisible world. The musicians can also protect others.

The Minianka musician is truly the psychologist, the psychiatrist, the caregiver of his people. His knowledge includes understanding the functioning of the different systems of the human body. Since he is sending sounds that affect people's bodies, he needs to know how the effects can be beneficial. When plants are needed to bring balance, he is ready to use them. The healing herbs and healing combinations of sounds are understood as intrinsically related.

MUSIC AND HEALING

Some village musicians may actually spend more time looking for precious herbs than playing their instruments. The example of Minianka musicians in small, materially poor villages who live up to the true purpose of their calling as people of healing knowledge is inspiring.

Music in the Minianka culture covers a whole range, from the music of joy to funerary music, from religious music to magical music. Its practice is based on psychological insight, diagnostic acumen, and understanding the impact of sound on people. It implies the study of plants for the protection of oneself and others. Often the development of divinatory powers is held to be a part of the musician's calling.

Music develops the power of memory because it is not written. The musicians have special herbal powders they use to facilitate memory and overcome performance anxiety. As guardians of the musical and herbal legacy, they are especially needed by the community. They protect morality. If they fail in their religious duties, they believe that the whole community can suffer. Thus, they bear important responsibilities.

Nangape

Once I saw my teacher Nangape treat a man who claimed he could transform himself into many shapes and appearances from one minute to the next. His body movements and gestures were agitated and irregular. He was violent, and I feared he would kill Nangape.

Nangape played the balafon, chanted, and prayed. Slowly, over a period of time, the patient became less agitated; the number of imaginary transformations diminished. Eventually, he could sit quietly, greet people normally. He still tends to be moody and at times aggressive toward whoever happens to cross his path, but he has been reintegrated successfully into the community as a former fool. After his treatments were completed, he was able to marry and to raise children. Nangape went through so many trials to treat this man that it was the case that most impressed me.

A Young Girl and the Healing Drum

In North America, I have occasionally used the healing drum with success in a few cases that have come my way. I had some friends from one of the Caribbean islands who were very well educated in the Western sense and proud of their achievements and social standing. They favored Western psychiatrists and psychologists over black folk religions. They regarded this aspect of their African heritage as demoniacal and to be avoided.

One of their daughters performed well in school until the age of seven. After that, she started having certain troubles. Listening to music, she would cry out and jump about. She started sucking her thumb and making infantile gestures. She urinated in bed, laughed and cried unexpectedly and exaggeratedly. Her body trembled when she was around music. The parents hid the child from others and tried to compensate by pushing her development and giving her intensive courses. The more they forced her, the more she forgot, including the alphabet. By the age of eight, she was labeled maladjusted, then mentally retarded. Her crises were especially provoked by the sound of music.

The parents decided to return to the island of their origins to seek out help for their daughter. Another factor in the decision was their belief that their social status would be threatened if their employers in North America knew about the girl. They hoped to find more tolerance on the island. They went to a psychiatrist of their country who had worked in Africa. He told them that in Africa he had observed certain cases of what is called possession that his modern methods were ineffective in healing, but that the traditional African healers could cure. He suggested their daughter might be better helped in this way.

They consulted a voodoo priest who informed them that in Montreal there was an African who could surely help them with their problems. He did not tell them who this was. They came back to Canada.

At the time I was giving dance classes, and they came with the child to see me. She understood the rhythms. She did not do the steps I was teaching to others, but she made up her own that went with the music. She also laughed in her peculiar way. The parents tried to show her the steps I was teaching. I told them not to mix themselves in this, that I would take care of it.

The girl would not move her arms and legs as I indicated. Her body moved as if it were remotely controlled by something. The parents wanted to work with the girl's will power, but I was not sure it was her own will that was refusing the movements. I had some intuitions about her resistance. I would play. She would move as she wanted. With my drumming I could push her further in what she was doing.

I told the parents, "You can trust me. Whatever she does, I can accept it, and I will keep it strictly confidential. What has happened to your family could happen to anyone. I have had worse things in my life. It is not the end of the world for me." This reassured them.

There were two cases of sickness before me. The parents, with their paranoia about their social standing, suffered from the first illness. The girl, who was embarrassing them, suffered from the second. The parents no longer invited anyone to their home. They avoided social contacts. I had to work on both cases of illness before me.

"What good is your social standing?" I reasoned with the parents. "If you have friends who cannot accept your ill child, then kick them out the door. If your love for your child is not stronger than that, put her in an asylum for the mentally retarded, and your conscience will be at peace. That is all. Your child was well; now she isn't. Does that change how you feel about her? Suppose that one of your other children loses an arm. What will you do? Will you stop loving her because she has become abnormal? Where is your parental conscience if you say a child is yours, but you do not love her if she is not the way you would like her to be?"

In my work with the girl herself, I began hesitantly, feeling my way along. I beat the drum to see at what point she would become afraid, at what point move. I hit some notes. She leaped up. Her body shook. Her movements were violent. I had awakened something that was sleeping in her, it seemed. I felt I should continue, because if I did not awaken it here, it would awaken of its own in the subway or some other inappropriate place. As I played, her movements became more and more violent. She shook all over, ran about, ran into walls, banged her head. Her parents wanted me to stop for fear she would kill herself. I told them to let me continue. After some time, the trembling ceased. The movements became more regular. I felt the girl herself was controlling her movements. I played, and she danced for three hours.

On the following day, I met with her again. She laughed only once, but without exaggeration. The sounds of the preceding day gave no results. So I played normally just to enjoy myself. Suddenly she started to dance. There was some violence in her movements, but it was not as prolonged as on the prior occasion. I followed her dance with my drumming.

We had a number of sessions like that. They became more normal. The girl no longer laughed out abnormally. Her bedwetting stopped. She listened when spoken to. Within two weeks, she could sit at the table and serve herself. When asked to write a letter of the alphabet, she did it correctly, whereas before, she would not even pick up a piece of chalk. She no longer sucked her thumb. I told her parents to keep me informed. If everything continued to go well, the work was done. If not, they could let me know. I could write to my mother for advice on which herbs would help stabilize her condition.

This was a successful case. I do not claim to have known the solution right away; I was simply attentive, as I had been taught to be. I observed carefully and let my intuition work.

Ceremony of the Ancestors

Now I sometimes find myself with five patients at the apartment. They sit there looking at one another and at times argue over trifling jealousies and rivalries. One case started to get very dangerous and presented quite a delicate problem. This particular patient came every day to where I worked and made threats that he wanted to kill people. His story was very complex. The difficulties had started back in Africa.

In the village he came from, there were two families who had a special relationship. One of the families was marked by a hereditary disease. When a family member fell sick with the disease, according to the local belief, to cure it required the human sacrifice of a member of the other family. He belonged to the family of the sacrificial victims. Some of his brothers and sisters had been used for sacrifices. The man I knew had grown up in the fear that he would be taken one day. In Montreal, his psychological problems started to show up.

Although he had left his country of origin and was living in Canada, the man could not completely forget the fear that had made such an impression on his childhood. Nonetheless, while growing up, he had known a boy from the other family, and they had gotten along well enough with each other. When this person

166

came to Montreal, the two friends arranged to live together, despite their bizarre family connection.

Everything went well until the day that my friend discovered some blood in the bathroom. One of the signs of the hereditary disease was abundant bleeding. The old fear was stirred up.

My friend thought, "He has the hereditary disease. He came here to sell my soul," which also means making a human sacrifice. "They have killed others in my family. Now they followed me here to take me as their victim." He did not dare to tell others about his obsession, but he confided in me.

His fear increased to the point that he bought a gun and drew up a list of people he needed to kill in order to feel safe. He listed the names of the members of the other family, a number of prominent Catholics, such as a Cardinal who often went to Africa, and the Pope, (this was because the family was Catholic), and, for some reason, President Reagan. He came each day at lunchtime to where I was working. He cried and shouted about all the people he would kill, especially the Catholics. Two priests among my colleagues began to feel threatened.

He was treated and released from a psychiatric hospital. While some of his symptoms diminished, he was unable to work. He was still possessed by fear, and he came to me for help. I invited him to come to my home for a healing ceremony. I asked two of my friends to assist me, a young Moroccan Jew who plays guitar in my group and a friend from Guinea. We would perform the Ceremony of the Ancestors.

I cautioned my ill friend, "You asked me to help you, to treat you. If you lie, you die. That is the condition."

I gave some money to buy red wine and candles. Alcohol was required for the ceremony. Commercial candles were not adequate for our purpose, so we got the only religiously consecrated candles available. They were marked "Israel." We filled a calabash with water. In the Ceremony of the Ancestors, we always offer some water to the ancestors to drink. The three others placed their left hands over the water. I wanted to see if our disturbed friend was possessed by a water spirit, which is very common on an island such as Montreal. I began to play the balafon while they left their hands over the water. Within a half hour, our ill friend was trembling, indicating possession. The others remained calm.

I needed to verify that the man was not epileptic. We lit four candles, one for each participant. The candle in front of the sick man went out. The other candles continued to shine. I played some music again. He did not react like an epileptic to the flickering candle light. Whatever was disturbing him was something different.

I asked him why his candle had gone out. He then asked one of my friends to light it, which he did right away with no difficulty. The other friend asked why he was not capable of lighting his own candle. So the sick friend blew it out and relit it himself.

I said, "All right, now we know what you are suffering from. You are a liar first of all."

"Yes," he admitted.

I continued, "You do not like anyone's friendship. He lit that candle out of friendship for you. You blew it out to prove yourself. Proving yourself, that is your problem. You did not even appreciate his gesture toward you. If you were normal, you would have said, 'Well, I could light it, but since he lit it in friendship, it is not necessary to do it again.' Something is not right. You are overwhelming people. I told you not to lie here."

He got down on his knees and said, "Pardon me."

"You owe your excuses to a whole society which you have disturbed," I told him. "By your behavior, you can persuade people that you are not crazy."

By gazing into the water my friend from Guinea was able to divine various things about the patient's life and ask him revealing questions. During our questioning, it came out that the patient thought he was impotent. "Do you think yourself impotent? Is that what triggered your problems? Is that why you want to kill humanity?"

"You are not an orphan either," I said to him. "You could have gone to Africa to speak with the elders about your problem. They would have found a solution. Instead of doing that, you menaced the world."

He asked to be excused and then he cried. I played the balafon again. It had taken us from five in the evening until one in the morning to reach this point. I spoke to him to deprogram his mind of all the negativities. The remedy was for him to discover the nature of his problem.

On the following day, he returned. I played the balafon again for him. He listened, lay down, and eventually went to sleep.

Within two weeks, he was working at a restaurant. He no longer needed psychiatric attention. He was no longer on the streets with the hoboes. He no longer wanted to kill anyone. His problem had been an inability to face the truth. Once he had it in front of him, he could not pretend any more.

My friend from Guinea has a gift, a clairvoyance. He asked probing questions while I concentrated on playing the notes and rhythms of the balafon that would calm the nerves of the disturbed man. With the Ceremony of the Ancestors, there is no fooling around. The ancestors will punish a liar. It is not a moment to irritate them. It is a time to get into harmony with everyone. The music created a peaceful, harmonious atmosphere among us. Because of it, evil spirits could not disturb any of us. Humans are strong when united. Spirits are frightened by union among people.

Nyama: The Slow Madness

Another phenomenon the Minianka healer musicians treat is known to them by the Bambara word *nyama*. In Bambara, this means ordure. There is a song about nyama, which states that everything becomes ordure, but ordure can never become everything. In Minianka, the meaning of the word nyama changed. Some informants say it means remorse. Others believe that it refers to a malefic power. Still others claim it refers virtually to the soul of a person. The word has many meanings.

When a Minianka hunter is about to shoot an animal, he feels obliged to say a prayer to chase away the nyama of the animal so that it will not be able to reach him. Before butchering the fallen animal, he speaks to it again. It is believed that certain spirits incarnate in animals to provoke human hunters. When such animals are shot at, the nyama immediately attacks the hunter.

If anyone takes the life of a human being, the nyama of the victim haunts the killer, who is no longer a normal person. Dogs and monkeys are held to have very strong nyamas. The hunter of a monkey must never let its body touch his head when he is transporting it on his shoulder. If this happens, the Minianka believe, the Nyama of the monkey will possess the hunter, and he will behave like a monkey.

Soldiers who have been to war and have killed are haunted by the nyama of their victims. Similarly, anyone who has an abortion is pursued by the nyama of the human being that was incarnating in the embryo. At the moment of conception, all the necessary elements for forming a human life are already present, according to the Minianka view. These are the double, the breath, and the beginnings of the body. Therefore, abortion is equivalent to killing a person who has already been born.

The Minianka developed a means of dealing with the hauntings of nyama. It involves a special ceremony for separating the person from the nyama. Music is played, and herbal potions are used to give further protection. An amulet may be worn afterwards.

Hunters and butchers who frequently kill animals are held to be prone to hauntings by the nyama of slain animals. They need special ceremonies to separate them from the nyama. From the Minianka viewpoint, anyone who has taken a human life becomes very imbalanced through the phenomenon of nyama. The result can be further danger to others. In the village, even woodcutters are given special care with regard to nyama, as their profession inevitably involves disturbing the lives of many creatures.

One characteristic of the nyama disorder is lack of a sense of what is important in life, failure to distinguish between the significant and the banal. The ill person tends to retreat into isolation. No activities are felt to have any value. Life itself seems without meaning. The person can find nothing fulfilling and does not even know what could be. The very will to make an effort is lacking. In the Minianka language, this is known as the "slow madness." In Western terminology, we might speak of depression, alienation, anomie. This is the inward manifestation of an essentially destructive orientation to life. Outward manifestations can vary. One example is pyromania, which the Minianka see as characteristic of one category of nyama sufferers. Another category involves people who go unnoticed until the day they commit a violent crime that surprises those who know them.

A part of the rehabilitation from nyama involves a reorientation to the dignity of life, a call to a respect for life as the primary value. Music, counseling, and herbs can work together toward a freeing from remorse and a reinfusing of purpose.

Hunter of Souls

For the Minianka, any activities involving crowds of people are carefully watched over by the elders and musicians responsible for the health of the people. For the Minianka, it is wiser to take precautions in these collective contexts than to have to suffer the consequences or heal the victims afterward. They interpret news of riots at soccer stadiums or shootings at carnivals in terms of the human vulnerability to invisible forces. When solidarity is lost due to negative emotions, people become susceptible to the "hunter of souls."

Once extremes of behavior are unleashed, normal restraints are not easily restored. Therefore, whenever there is a popular celebration in the Minianka village, the musicians take measures so that the hunter of souls cannot enter the circle. The elders are always notified before music is to be played. Nowadays, because of a breakdown of traditional discipline, festivals are most often celebrated next to the blacksmith's forge. The anvil is still considered the most powerful of purifying fetishes in the village. People seek its protection. The evil intentions of sorcerors can have no effect near the anvil.

The kinds of madness encountered in Africa have become more complex due to the mixing of the Western and African cultures. Many people are not armed for living in both worlds. Even if they have received diplomas, they have not assimilated the profound values of Western culture. They may use electronics without any understanding of the motivations of its inventors to dominate nature. At the same time, they are either ignorant or ashamed of their African heritage. The rate of mental illness has increased. Patients shuttle between the psychiatrists in the cities and the healers in the villages without finding cures. Effective methods need to be found for dealing with current problems. We have to start all over again.

13

TWO CULTURES

After my year in Sikasso, I was promoted to the high school in Bamako, the capital city. In Bamako, the work really began. That is when I started to feel the implications of Western civilization.

In Sikasso, I had still been able to walk barefoot in the streets. As a boarder at the school in Bamako, I had to eat with fork and knife seated at a table. Salad was served. I had to eat it. It was hard. To me, green leaves like that were food for goats, not humans. I was in a dormitory and no longer lived with an African family. Lentils, bread, and coffee were served in the morning. I could not make noise. Everything was regimented. The school officials called newcomers like me "blues." They gave us towels, soap, shoes. I did not know how to wear shoes like that or tie the laces. The students from the city hazed us, calling us bush people, savages with hard stomachs but nothing in our brains.

This was just at the time when Mali became an independent republic. It was a difficult period of transition. I had to learn so many new things, including how to go to the movies and how to dance the twist. In music class, I had to listen to Beethoven and Vivaldi. The teacher would play a symphonic selection and ask the students to identify the composer and write about the piece. I did not understand very well, and the dance class was surely the worst.

There was peer pressure to put on sophisticated airs, to appear arrogant. Vulgar language was in fashion. It was expected that we say "shit" and "I don't give a damn" to everyone. In the village, an attitude of "I don't give a damn" was considered inhuman. Our traditional values taught us that everything human was our concern. These cynical attitudes of the city went against the deepest principles of my culture. In order to pass as cool and tough, we even had to take nicknames, like Django, or something else from an American Western.

The administration expected me to become a little Frenchman. I found myself wedged between this model of behavior and the badly raised style current among many students. Because of my village dweller's spirit, I tended to reject arbitrary impositions that went against my customs. So I was often punished along with the "I don't give a damn" crowd, even though I did not emulate them. When I did not feel like putting on laced shoes, I did not wear them. Similarly, if I felt like eating with my hands, as we do in the village, I did so.

For such infractions, I was sent each time to the school's disciplinary council. They questioned whether I was at school to become civilized and punished me with solitary enclosure in the room we students called the dungeon. At noon, they told us to take a nap. When I was not sleepy, I chatted with other students. I was ordered to shut up. This was so different from village life, where there had always been animated conversation, drumming, the sounds of life. Even at night in the village there was talking and socializing. Naturally, I tried to continue this custom at school but kept running up against imposed discipline that was foreign to my nature.

In the village, when educators heard youth expressing themselves obscenely, they always intervened and insisted on decent speech. In this high school, it was different. The students expressed themselves in the worst possible language, and the teachers did not object. They even used such vulgar expressions themselves. I wondered how these adults could be considered well educated.

Gamma Zero

Because of my regular appearances before the disciplinary council, I received a nickname: Gamma Zero. In the language of physics, this meant no speed, zero acceleration. The implication was that with respect to civilization I was starting from scratch. A boy from the city claimed that my presence in the same class with him brought down his value. He wanted to change class. A group tried to persuade me to resign from the high school. Fate was following me, it seemed.

This particular boy persisted in seeking out ways to unbalance me. No matter what I did, he criticized and discounted it. He called me "little savage," "little Minianka," "dog eater," and "Gamma Zero."

I had learned in my age group in the village that when other boys tried to give a nickname, the name would stick if one reacted to it negatively. I remembered this lesson from village life and showed no signs of discomfort.

At every opportunity, he taunted and belittled me. I started to feel like putting an end to all this. He stopped me in town one day, and in front of my cousin, who went to the girls' high school, he said, "You know, I am telling you that you are going to quit school, leave this city, and go back to your accursed village."

I answered, "Only God knows."

Finally, one day I was sitting with some friends when he crossed the limit. He mentioned my mother: "Does your mother dare to say that she brought a child into the world?"

It was time to put an end to his game. I felt fire in my middle. My limbs weakened. I was burning. I left my friends and said I was ill.

The next time I saw him was in the cafeteria. He began with his taunts. "When I speak to you, open your mug and answer," he said.

I kept silent and burned.

He repeated, "Are you opening your mug?"

I told him, "You and I will die together today."

He mocked me, "You're puffed up with pride, huh? You're threatening me? I can finish you off in one movement right here."

I told him, "No, it will not be so simple as that. This evening we will die together. You say you will be going today to the soccer field by the big hotel. I'll be waiting for you."

When the moment of confrontation arrived, he tried to back down. "Listen," he said, "I was just joking around."

I said, "You joked around too much."

He asked, "Why didn't you say anything about it?"

I informed him, "You went too far. Your mother never taught you any limits."

He said, "Excuse me."

I said, "It's too late."

He protested, "Listen, I was just having fun."

I said, "You were having fun at my expense, and you find that funny. Why did you say the name of my mother?"

He reacted, "Oh, is that all? Well, excuse me."

"It is too late," I repeated. "I did not come here for dialogue with you."

Energized by all the accumulated hatred, I knocked him senseless with one blow to the head. The police came to pick him up. To this day, I do not know where he is. We never saw him again in the high school.

The title Gamma Zero had left its traces on me. I wondered in those high school years in Bamako if I had been misplaced in the city environment. I saw the city boys on their motorbikes, going to the movies, listening to Johnny Holiday on their sound systems, wearing stylish European clothes. On weekdays the sense of dislocation was not so severe, because no one went out. On Saturday evening, however, the sadness began. I had no money to go to the movies. I sat in the dormitory but did not feel like studying. At best, I could stroll down the streets with a few friends like me. Without identity cards, though, we would have been arrested if the police had stopped us. These cards were a European custom left over from the colonial days. We went out secretively at times to hear the indigenous people of Bamako play their traditional music on balafon and drums. We feared being seen by our classmates who went to parties at embassies or did other things with snob appeal.

Even though this was after independence, our minds were still colonized. France represented the ideal. We were ashamed of the dust that got on our clothes and bodies when we went to listen to the balafon. On returning to the dormitory, we would try to wash quickly before the others could question us too closely about where we had been. Personally, I was too weakened by the previous rejections I had suffered to resist the attitudes of the assimilated Africans, who wanted to deny who they were in their imitation of the white people.

THE HEALING DRUM

Fortunately, at school we had theater and folkloric dance productions. I often participated in these as a drummer and dancer, thereby having at least one outlet through which to express myself rhythmically.

The worst that happened to me and others like me in this ambivalent ambiance is that we learned to be ashamed of our mothers, to detest them. When I went to bed, I would say to myself, "Here I am, Yaya, who is intelligent in this high school, who has succeeded in spite of everything. All I have is a poor, dirty, little mother who sleeps in a room in a round hut in an African village. I am ashamed." In retrospect, that I ever felt this way about my mother is the greatest shame, the greatest wound in my life. The systematic brainwashing to which I was exposed from the first day of elementary school to reject my origins was the sole cause of it.

In Bamako, my city-dwelling classmates sometimes invited me to their homes to meet their parents. They would say to me that one day they wanted to visit my village. I did not dare invite them to my home. When they asked me where I came from, I did not even admit that I came from the village of Fienso. Rather, I said I was from Koutiala, because it is a bigger town. In the stereotyped thinking of the time, a village such as Fienso was associated with uncivilized, animistic, uneducated eaters of dogs. My pretense was quickly unmasked when my friends asked me if I was acquainted with certain well-known individuals from Koutiala. I always had to say no. They caught on quickly that I was a boy from the bush.

The wound came when a friend announced he would visit me at my home. I went so far as to succumb to the temptation of telling him that my mother was dead. I pretended the woman he would meet was a mean stepmother. At the time, I felt a clear conscience to deny my own mother, whom I love in my depths. Her only fault was to have put me into the world with my intelligence, which had brought me into a milieu where she seemed inadequate. When the boy came, my mother served him without any special ceremony the cereal porridge we are accustomed to eating as a staple food. He looked at it and said it was food that would not even be served to a dog where he came from.

When my mother observed that he would not eat, she said, "Return to the city. There is nothing for you here."

I accompanied him. She felt my discomfort and sensed I was

Figure 10. Yaya Diallo's mother, Tompéquè Berthé, stands in the midst of women of the Niewoh society.

ashamed of her. She accepted it in quiet dignity, never held it against me or talked to me about it. I respect her for this.

Coredjouga

My mother is what we call *coredjouga*. This means a person who has shed everything, who has no need for material possessions. Coredjouga can be translated as scavenger. The coredjouga knows how to make do with scraps and feels no contempt for anything. Material things do not matter for the coredjouga, whose role in society is to educate others through irony. While making people laugh, the coredjouga also educates them.

My mother plays this role, which includes being the interpreter

177

and intermediary between the society and the traditional chief. Through humor, the coredjouga are moderating influences in the community. They are very good dancers who dare to move freely in ways that would be considered bold and shameless for other people. They make the villagers laugh with their swinging hips when they dance as if they are being sexually alluring. This is what is on people's minds, though, and the dances are intended to give lessons. The coredjouga are such good dancers that at times they purposefully make it look as if they are dancing badly. People wonder how it is possible to dance so terribly, and the effect is very humorous.

On one of my trips to Fienso in the 1980s, I saw a perfect example of how the coredjouga work. I had just arrived with some visitors from Quebec. We went to the village square and sat in the circle with the villagers who were gathered for the evening's relaxation. An old musician moved around the circle while playing a drum. His job was to ensure that the spirits of the place would be pacified. A coredjouga also stalked around amusingly, wearing the distinctive necklace of the coredjouga, which lies over one shoulder, crosses the body diagonally, and goes under the opposite arm. He was responsible for calming the children. My mother has retired from this particular function.

Two children started to fight. The coredjouga approached them and asked what was happening.

The first child said, "He insulted me."

The coredjouga asked, "Was it a new insult he invented?"

"He insulted my mother," the offended boy complained.

"Oh, that is an old insult," laughed the coredjouga. "It has never killed anyone here. I would have worried if it were a new insult. That one is nothing to worry about. We have tested all the old insults, and they are harmless. Look around you. All of these people you see have been insulted, but they are fine. Enjoy yourself."

The child sat down peacefully. The problem was resolved.

My son Telli surprised the villagers in Fienso in 1988 when he started dancing to the drums in the breakdancing style he had learned in Canada. They were astonished. "Where did he learn that?" they asked. To them, he looked like a coredjouga dancer. The villagers laughed. In our language, we call this the dance of the badly raised child. My mother proudly claimed credit, however, and said Telli took after her in his dancing. In the West, breakdancing was a new style. To us, it is an old thing. The same movements that made one a good dancer in the West showed one was improperly educated, or pretending to be, in our village.

My mother is content in her role of coredjouga. My brothers and sisters and I have given her new clothing, but she will never wear it. She is happy with her old clothes. She walks about sometimes with the top half of her body uncovered and a simple cloth wrapped in the traditional fashion around her waist and going down to her ankles. According to our customs, this is perfectly suitable attire. My mother is uninfluenced by either the Western or the Islamic attitudes about dress. The fact that people come from faraway villages to consult with her for her knowledge has not changed her one bit.

My sisters used to feel ashamed to see our mother walk about half-naked. She refused to be changed from her habits. She explained, "We have suffered so much. I do not want to provoke jealousy by dressing in a fancier fashion. Do I want to look like someone who is trying to attract a new husband by making myself look more beautiful? I have no need for that. You are young. Dress up as you like. It is your time to be concerned with the exterior aspect of life. That season is past for me. In my tattered rags, I shall pass the rest of my life."

My brothers and sisters and I gave my mother a modern bed with a mosquito net for her comfort at night. She sleeps next to it on a thin, straw mat on the floor.

When others come to visit her, my mother accepts them, one and all, regardless of how they are dressed or of whether they are scrubbed clean or grimy from their travels and labors. She tells us, her children, "Life is not a matter of external things. If you do not understand me now, perhaps you will after my death."

Assimilation

In high school, I admit, I was flattered to be considered intelligent in the white system. Having been labeled an idiot in my village, I welcomed the change in the estimate of my abilities. I was motivated to prove I merited this positive recognition. During my years in high school I was ranked second only three times; the rest of the time I was first in my class. I could accept people calling me socially and culturally backward, but I had a real taste for scholastic laurels. The second highest academic rank was not good enough for my ambitions.

I did not learn by rote, rather, I learned to reflect on problems and to trust in my aptitude for solving them by thinking. Many other students sought to solve problems by similitude, based on other cases they had practiced. This never excited me. My musical training in the village had taught me to observe and reflect. I was able to apply these skills to academic work also.

Mali's independence came during my high school years. After French domination and discipline, we had the Malian regime of socialism. We were supposed to practice self-discipline. The idea was that a student militia would police the rest of the students. A government minister accompanied by troops of soldiers came to announce the new system to us. Many students were dissatisfied with the new plan—we wanted discipline to be enforced by someone who knew what the word was supposed to represent. How could they expect undisciplined youth like us to discipline ourselves? We did not even know the new rules they wanted us to conform to. A militia would have created divisions among us and caused us to denounce our friends. This was contrary to the village system of solidarity among members of an age group. In our discussions, we students decided to say no to the government. I thought there was unity among us on this.

As the government minister addressed the assembled students, I could not contain myself and called out, "We do not agree!"

No one else joined in and supported me. I looked around. I stood alone.

The minister asked, "Did someone say something?"

I announced, "I do not agree!"

Soldiers surrounded me, grabbed me, kicked me, and took me to military camp for one month of punishment. When they released me to go back to school, they warned me that if I opposed government programs, I would disappear, which was a euphemistic way of saying that they would kill me.

It was a difficult transition period. The new government oriented itself to Marxist ideas. The major world powers were competing for influence in the young African nations. One way they sought to impress our educated youth who might one day become leaders was to offer prizes at graduation for outstanding achievements in high school. The embassies of France, the United States, the Soviet Union, and China gave prizes for merit in letters, mathematics, history, discipline, and other fields. Since the embassy officials had no direct contact with the students, the prizes were placed in the hands of the high school administrators, who were trusted to choose appropriate individuals for the awards.

The assistant principal in charge of discipline chose me to receive the Lenin Prize for self-discipline. He commended me for the accomplishment of having been able to bring order into a class that had previously been found impossibly unruly. In doing this, I had simply been holding true to values I was taught in my village, namely, that one remains quiet in the presence of an elder brother. I was insistent on this with my fellow students, and they responded to my appeals on the basis of traditional values. Somehow, the school officials had misunderstood my motivation and thought I was moved by the socialist ideal of self-discipline. Considering the public stand I had earlier taken against a student militia and my subsequent punishment, I was, to say the least, amazed by the irony of my becoming the recipient of this prize for self-discipline.

It seems that another aspect of my behavior at high school had also been misunderstood. In informal discussions with fellow students, as well as in classes, whenever the occasion arose, I spoke in support of African values and against the incursions of Western civilization. I was being true to my beliefs and my African peasant origins. The authorities apparently mistook me for being an anticapitalist revolutionary. But I did not care for the Marxism we were taught in class. "Workers of the world, unite" said nothing to me. I was not worried about the world, just about my culture. Consequently, I never read a bit of the seven thick volumes on Marxism that I received as my prize.

Throughout high school, I continued to defend who I was, resisting those who would change me. Despite academic success, I did not make fast progress in becoming acculturated to the European model of social demeanor. I was stable, like a tree that was not moving anywhere.

A Scholarship

During my final year in high school, at the Easter vacation period, the school gave the students intelligence tests. I felt disinterested and hardly reflected as I checked off my answers. This is made for intelligent people, I thought; what does it matter to me?

In the second week that I was back in school after the holidays, I was called to the government scholarship office. I arrived and sat down among others. An official came and called, "Mr. Diallo."

I wondered why I was being addressed formally like that and started to feel fear.

The man spoke to me, "As it turns out, you have an above-average intelligence. In fact, you are a genius."

I had gotten used to being an idiot. Now I was responsible for being a genius. It actually changed my identity in the high school. He told me I was being given a scholarship to study sanitary engineering in Canada.

I asked, "What is that, sanitary engineering?"

He answered, "Evidently, it is medicine."

He based this deduction on the fact that the French word *sanitaire* refers to measures taken to maintain health. This was the first time that Mali had constituted an office to give scholarships. The officials did not know the meaning of some of the presumed specializations in the foreign universities. I had friends sent to study, "cadastral engineering." Neither they nor the deans in their new institutions could even figure out in what school of the university they were supposed to be registered.

The news of my new status and the scholarship weighed on me heavily. I slept poorly. "The country is counting on me," I reflected. It was a new challenge. I was accustomed to situations in which people had no confidence in me. This was different—they believed in me. I had serious problems with it.

At this time something else happened to me. In my village, it was interpreted that a female spirit was in love with me. Each time that a woman was proposed for marriage with me, she died. It happened twice. One woman was proposed to me, and shortly afterwards she drowned. After the second loss, the adults in charge of arranging marriages stopped proposing anyone for me. These sad occurrences added weight to my decision to go study in Canada.

The attachment of this feminine spirit to me seemed to affect me on certain days of the week and especially for three days at the time of the full moon. I would become more aggressive and had to watch myself closely and not get too involved with others. Some days I was fine. On other days, my thoughts were confused. Here was one more reason for classifying me a fool.

I completed the baccalaureate and was in the first class to receive Malian, instead of French, diplomas. We did not yet know what value these diplomas would have in the eyes of foreign universities.

When I returned to the village afterwards, my family questioned me: "It seems you finished school in Bamako this year. What are you going to do now? Will you go to work?"

I responded, "No."

"What then?" they insisted.

I said, "I am waiting."

"For what?" they asked.

I went to work in the fields at home until one day a nurse from a nearby village came by to say he had heard my name on the broadcast notices on the radio. I was being called to Bamako. The family asked me why I was being called over the radio. I explained that I would be sent to one of the white people's countries to study some more. I had to borrow money from someone else just to get to Bamako, because my family did not want to give me any.

A Chemist in Canada

I was sent to Canada. There I was told I would be in the engineering school of the University of Montreal to study sanitary engineering for industrial design. That was not my interest, however. Perhaps preparation for a career in pharmacy or as a biology professor would have suited me better. At least those studies would have involved me with plants, which were traditionally of interest in my family, and which I had learned about and loved in the village. In engineering school, the courses were taught in French, but the textbooks were in English. It took a lot of time to study.

The Canadian government warned me, "If you fail one subject because you are undisciplined, we will kick you out."

A problem arose in one physics course. They ordered me to return to my country. I argued with them, "I will not return to my country. I came here to study, and I am going to study."

This occurred after two and a half years in the engineering school, with two and a half left for the completion of my degree. Instead of leaving, I transferred to the chemistry department.

I imagined that as a chemist I would be able to study the healing properties of plants. I went to work in a factory to support myself while I studied chemistry.

For four years my presence in Canada was illegal. I worked and studied but had no papers. When my engineering scholarship was cut off the officials gave me an airline ticket for my return to Mali. I tore it up and threw it in the trash.

Then Canada offered clemency to all illegal aliens. We were invited to announce our presence and go to the immigration office to put our situation in order. I heard this and decided to cooperate.

After numerous bureaucratic entanglements, which nearly resulted in my deportation, the Minister of Immigration interceded for me, and I received my legal papers.

With my legal papers in hand, I presented myself to the chemistry department of the University of Montreal to seek employment. I was successful in my search, but that is where a new set of problems started. I worked with a Frenchman to develop waterproof paper. Our project was not just to find a process for coating one surface with a waterproof solution but how to make the paper waterproof through and through as it came off the production rollers. The more I worked, the more I liked chemistry. I brought home samples of the paper, and it impressed my friends, above all the Africans. They were proud that my African brains were involved in high technology.

They encouraged me, "Yes, learn such techniques, and with that we will develop Africa."

I had risen to a new identity: well dressed, a big researcher, going out with the most desirable girls. The roles had changed. In my entourage, my title of research assistant at the university had high status.

The paper I was developing was used in the navy and the army— and by the police to give tickets while it was raining or snowing. This did not agree with my values. I did not like the idea of the paper's being used for military strategy or to give tickets to people.

I found a new job in a laboratory. One aspect of my work consisted of determining the future availability of underground water at sites in Israel and other desert countries. I thought that at least this was work that could be useful for Mali.

I did not question this job until the day I looked at my director and wondered, "Did my mother bring me into the world to become a man like him? Is this my reason for living?" I started having serious problems with this. Nothing was wrong with the director himself, he just did not reflect back to me a role model with whom I could identify. I was saturated with doing work that did not fulfill my dream. But what was my dream?

The Healing Drum

By coincidence, at about this time a nun came from Africa to teach religious studies. She wanted to take a group of students to a camp with some Africans for one reason or another. Someone spoke to her about me, saying that I came from a small village, and if I took off my tie I could tell them some stories. She rang my doorbell to invite me to the camp. I had been planning to go out dancing with a fashionable lady. Nonetheless, I accepted the invitation to the camp.

Some of the young people had brought drums. I stood there in my suit and necktie and listened to some Africans acting as if they could play. This pretense irritated me. I knew what good playing was. I walked over, took a drum and played myself.

They were surprised, "Yaya, you have hidden talents?"

To me, this was my nature, not hidden talents. Underneath, though, I felt insecure. I feared I would fall back into Gamma Zero status. I mumbled something about having a bit of a heritage from my grandfather and retreated behind my necktie.

Because I was no longer used to drumming, my hands had softened. As a result, the playing I did at the camp left me with blisters that interfered with the manual aspect of my laboratory work. I almost lost my job because of this. I asked myself more and more often, "What am I doing here with these test tubes and machines?"

One evening I was supposed to go out dancing with some friends. We planned on dressing up in our finest. Can you imagine the anomaly of a black man like me taking three hours to get dressed before going out? It was too much. Arranging the tie, looking in the mirror, combing the hair, changing the hair style to an Afro, flattening it down again. Three hours! Yet when I looked at myself, I still was not happy.

Then the phone rang. It was my date: "I don't know what to wear today. I feel too fat. My beautiful dress doesn't fit. I need to go on a diet. What suit are you wearing?"

I told her which suit I had on. She said it would not go with the color of her dress. So I had to change and start all over again. Preparations like this needed to start at seven so I could be ready to go out by ten or ten-thirty.

After the phone call, I noticed two maps I had put up on my wall. One was of West Africa. The other was a tourist map of my country, "Mali, Land of Welcome." I gazed at the picture on it of a boy whose hair was simply cut short and who had the most beautiful smile. I said to myself, "He looks happy. I think I was once happy like him. No, I don't think I was ever happy like him."

I went on talking to myself in this manner and looked at the maps. Suddenly, there was an inexplicable shift in my perception. The earth of the African continent became tangibly present to me. It emerged from the map, came toward me, reached my face, entered into my body, and filled me. I felt and saw this earth within me. Africa came to look for me there in Canada. It has never since let go of me.

My necktie started to feel too tight, to choke me. I said, "Why am I wearing this jacket, these things from the Champs-Élysées?" I tore them off—my shirt, my shoes; I threw them in the garbage. Finally I was naked like the boy on the map. I stayed like that. The door bell rang. I did not open the door.

From the other side, I heard a voice say, "I have come to get you."

I answered, "No, don't bother. I am not going out tonight."

She asked, "Are you angry with me?"

I said, "No."

"What happened?" she queried further.

I said, "Nothing."

She went to get my friend with his date. They came back together and rang the bell again. I opened the door, naked as I was.

"What, you're not dressed yet?" shrieked my date. "I called you to make sure you'd be ready. You must get dressed right away."

"No," I answered with determination, "I will not get dressed." Then I closed the door quickly with a "good night."

I went to work on Monday simply dressed, without a tie. I told my director I was quitting.

"You have a contract," he reminded me.

"But I am quitting," I insisted quietly.

He requested that I stay there a month to train my replacement. I accepted. It was the longest month of my life.

TWO CULTURES

The director tried to sympathize: "Are you tired? You can take a rest. We'll pay for you to have a vacation in the Bahamas."

I told him, "That is not the issue. I am not tired. I intend to play the drums."

He asked how I would support myself. The penalty for abandoning my job was that there would be no unemployment insurance. I accepted the situation. I had some savings. I bought myself a small conga and started to play.

My friends asked, "Is Yaya crazy?" By African custom, if someone becomes mentally disturbed, the friends must try to help. They kept asking me, "How are you doing? Is everything all right?"

I continued to answer, "Fine."

They were trying to figure out what was going on in my head. Finally, they approached me more directly, "Something is wrong. You must stop playing because it is not good for the reputation of the Malians here. You are the only Malian fooling around with drums." I told them I was not fooling around.

The Malians living in Canada called a meeting on the national level to deal with various problems they were having. I felt responsible to represent my people, the Minianka. To my surprise, the Case of Yaya was brought up. "Do you want to humiliate Mali here?" I was asked. "You were sent here to study in order to go back to help your country. This is called a lack of national conscience. Your parents and everyone else have paid taxes to educate you."

I objected to their use of the word educate: "To instruct me, yes. To educate me, no. I received my education in my village." I was thinking of all I had learned with Nangape, my mother, my age group, my initiation, and the secret societies.

They did not relent: "You were sent here to help your country to get out of underdevelopment. When Africans work overseas instead of in their country, this is called the brain drain, the escape of grey matter. In your case, it is the loss of grey matter. When you are playing drums, you no longer have any brain tissues. You are dishonoring your country. You play in the streets now, whereas you used to be a respected chemist here. You had arrived at making something out of your life, but now you have fallen into the stupidity of drums. Stop that. Go back to work."

The Malian consul himself suggested I get the help of a psychiatrist.

THE HEALING DRUM

I responded, "Listen. I insult your logic. I left Africa to come here to study, and instead of returning with a diploma, I return with a drum. Who understands that?"

They reproached me, "Do you even know how to play drums? You are lying to the white people that you know how to play."

I said, "If I am lying to people, that is my problem."

They taunted, "Will you play for the American Indians? Or perhaps will you go to the North Pole and play for the Eskimos?"

I told them, "That's none of your business. I quit my work, and I can tell you the same thing I told my employer. I do not want to be a laboratory technician for the rest of my life. I decided that is enough. I am more a musician than a chemist. That is what I know how to do the best. It is what I saw my ancestors doing. To be a chemist is anonymous. Anyone can get a diploma and say he is a chemist. I am the heir of something. It is not just anyone who has inherited it. I do not have the heritage of others. My conscience is awakened to my legacy, to what I have in my hand. I do not need to justify myself in front of you."

Still they told me I was lacking in conscience. Some who saw me on the street even called out, "Hey, man without a conscience!"

I became a solitary individual, a fool. I did not belong to anyone. I was unemployed, out of money. I tried to work with other musicians, without much success.

In those days, my mind was not quite there. I gave lessons at times for a couple of beers. I was even taken advantage of in this way. I recorded percussion in studios for records on which my name never appeared and was sent on my way with some beer. Those were the days when I got to know the hoboes of Montreal. Occasionally one will see me on the street and greet me: "Hi, we haven't seen you in quite a while."

Then one day, someone arrived in a red outfit with something hanging around his neck. He was a Rajneesh follower and wanted to learn to play the drums. I thought, oh no, he is not going to last long here. He spoke a lot about energy. He had seen me playing and found the energy was good. That is why he wanted to learn from me.

The man in red brought me to a turning point in my career. He said, "I want to produce a record for you."

I was incredulous. I told him, "Keep that to yourself. Do not tell anyone else. People will laugh at you and say that I am dreaming."

It was evident to me that the people I had been training were not at a level of competency to merit a record.

However, my student learned that it was technically possible for me to be my own accompanist. So I conceived the record accordingly. When the record became a reality in 1980, under the title of *Nangape*, in honor of my teacher, there were only two musicians on the record, myself and a flutist, Sylvain Leroux. I played first balafon, second balafon, and drums.

The record began to get some attention, and it surprised many people. Radio stations were playing it. *Downbeat* gave the record a very favorable review, and another jazz magazine, *Cadence,* also wrote an article on it. The record opened doors for me to teach and perform in the United States. I thanked my producer, Steve Conroy, and laughed at the irony of things: it took this obstinate Jewish man, a follower of an Indian guru on top of it, to launch my career in African music in North America. He accepted my thanks and said it was his way of giving something important to people.

Return to Mali

I returned to Mali with a package of twenty-five of the records for presents. It was fifteen years since I had first left for Canada, but this was not my first return. At the customs inspection in Mali, I lost five of the records, as each of the customs officers who saw them wanted one. I distributed them to friends and at the high school. There was excitement, "Hey, look at what Yaya did in North America."

Then a problem arose with the Malian Center for Rehabilitation, established because of the repatriation difficulties suffered by Malians who had studied abroad. The director, a friend of mine, assembled his committee, all teachers of what it is to be a Malian. I was called to appear before them but given no explanation. The director had told the committee they were to consider a very serious case.

When I arrived, one woman who knew nothing about my life began by criticizing me for rejecting traditional African culture.

I said nothing.

"Do we who are assembled here really want to be Malians?" asked my friend, the director. "What does this mean? Can our society accept a copatriot who has studied overseas but wants to be a Malian in the true sense of the word? The man whom you see here has been in a foreign country for twelve years. He is a graduate of our high school who never failed, who received a scholarship from us, which shows he is not an imbecile. He completed his university diploma and was working. When I traveled to Canada on a mission, I met him, ate in his home, went to a discotheque with him. He was not lacking in money and sent some back to his family. However, as he was not happy with his work, he quit his job. Since then he has been playing the djembe. Now when you visit his home, all you see are musical instruments. When he comes to Mali, he sleeps on the ground, speaks with the elders, chews cola nuts, and shows respect for all the villagers. When I went to bring him here, he was at his grandfather's, not in a villa or hotel."

The same woman who had criticized me now disapproved of my renunciation of Western-style success. "How are you going to feed your mother?" she asked.

Finally, my friend addressed her, "I am the director who invited this man here, but you misunderstand why. I have seen you adore, pardon, and try to readapt people who contemptuously treat you as backward. Yet you vomit on someone who, in the end, is more Malian than you. This is an examination of our conscience. What do we want in our society?"

I have been a serious case—for the Malian conscience. For all of the African intellectuals there today, I am an ill man, a fool, because I succeeded but then refused the success. One does not leap from civilization to fall into savagery—it is not the logical path. They say that even the white people passed through the primitive stage and then surpassed it. I had the chance to do this but rejected it. This upsets them to this day.

Three Cultures

Becoming Westernized is not easy: it takes perhaps twenty years of schooling and living experience. Although I spent seven years in the village school, I never even thought of throwing away my parents' traditions. And after seven more years of schooling in our capital city of Bamako, I still did not comprehend fully the new lifestyle being proposed to me. University studies and work as a chemist revealed the implications of westernization to me.

The Western influence is not spreading as rapidly in Africa as

Islam, and Islam causes me more fear for my endangered culture. I find it is possible to be in dialogue with people from the West, but conversion to Islam requires rejection of traditional beliefs and practices. People of my tribe who became Moslems had to kill what was African in themselves. In one day, they learned their prayers and were instructed to burn their drums and masks. Afterward they may have regretted the losses and realized they had not taken the time to reflect on what they were destroying, but it was usually too late.

I am not certain that the sort of conversion practiced in Mali can make good Moslems out of people, as it happens so quickly. Apprenticeship in anything takes time. The repetition of a prayer five times daily requires some discipline but does not make serious demands on people to understand. Yet the promise of an afterlife in paradise is very inviting.

The government is now supporting the Islamization of the country. Arab funding subsidizes the construction of a big mosque with loudspeakers in the capital. During the month of Ramadan, I no longer have the right to play the drums in the land of my birth. Although our country is peopled by Moslems, animists, and Christians, the Moslems are imposing their laws on all. They are not showing respect for the other cultures. The national radio station announces throughout the entire country the governmental edicts that prohibit music, ceremonies, amusements, and the opening of bars during the month of Ramadan. As Mali is not officially an Islamic republic, such an imposition makes no sense to me.

We Minianka pride ourselves on being those who refuse the master. Such a pro-Islamic government policy is especially hard on the traditionalists among us. To the government, our so-called resistance is problematical. They see us as persisting in refusing, but we are just persisting in being ourselves.

During my last visit to Mali, I met a countryman who said he was ready to walk to Saudi Arabia and live there as a slave just to have the privilege of dying in the holy land, which he thought would enhance his chances of going to paradise. It is not easy to understand that, in 1988, someone could think this way.

One of the popular methods in Mali of proselytizing for Islam involves distributing booklets profusely illustrated with pictures of people who are in hell for engaging in actions contrary to Islamic teachings. The pictures are persuasive and instill much fear.

THE HEALING DRUM

Another disturbing feature of the spread of Islam is the way the proselytizers take advantage of some of the fundamental values of our culture to undermine it. To our old people, for example, a proper burial and funeral are very important. At times, some of the younger generation convert to Islam first and then tell the elders they will not touch the corpses of heathen. The elders, for fear of not being decently buried, begin to say their Moslem prayers. I do not know where it is written in the Koran that a child who prays must not touch the corpse of his mother who has not prayed in the name of Allah. This seems to be a version of conversion peculiar to Africa.

Because I believe in my traditional culture, its erosion under the spread of Islam is disquieting. In the village of my mother's birth, Zangasso, the greatest initiator of the Komo secret society converted to Islam and sold the Komo fetish to a merchant who traffics in authentic African artifacts as if they were commodities with no sacred value. The initiator burned down the Komo hut and all the implements in it. The selling of the statue is itself a sacrilege and, as with slavery, both the seller and the buyer are wrong. If we read history, often only the buyers of the slaves were condemned; it is forgotten that many Africans profited by selling their fellows into the hands of the Western slavers. In the case of the Komo fetish, the Westerner who bought it would not have known where to look for it or what it was without the complicity of the initiator who forsook it.

Some people recognize the value of my abandoning my successful career to come back to our culture. I feel supported in the knowledge that my ancestors contributed to humanity through the music they played and taught, and that I am continuing their heritage.

14

THE HEALING
DRUM TODAY

By taking up the drums, I was able to heal the biggest wound I suffered from my experience of westernization: the shame I felt for my mother.

My mother is not one of those city women with their jewelry, embroidered gowns, and a stylish gait. She is not one to boast. She is a noble woman, but her nobility is not exterior. She is dignified and crawls before no one. Yet at night she sleeps on a small mat on the floor.

I respect my mother for the ferocious inner battle she fought to protect her children. Often she had to keep quiet in public, to efface herself. Privately, she counseled us, "Their hatred will end some day."

She also advised us that if we did something wrong, we should recognize it and simply excuse ourselves. That is only human. However, we should never bend before anyone, never ask for pity or for another chance. No human is the Creator; therefore we should accord no one that sort of power over us. Nor should we lie around waiting for happiness. It was up to us to find it in whatever happened to be our situation.

THE HEALING DRUM

On a recent visit to my mother, I saw that she is content that six of her children have survived and are living constructively. Our mother has been our example of tenacity, courage, and dignity. This has been a precious gift to us.

Today in the village, my mother is president of the women's secret society, Niewoh. She has friends and is respected. Some people travel from far away to sit by her and listen to her. All the village elders consult with her. She is patient with everyone. She taught me, "Leave others the chance to appreciate themselves." This sentence is the key to forgiveness. When my mother dies, the village of Fienso will be full of people who have come to honor her at her funeral. When her six living children come together, we have some weight in the proceedings of the village. She taught us values that came out of her strong, traditional African family background.

I felt ashamed of my mother until the day I took up the drums. As I played, I recognized her cultural wealth, which it is my privilege to carry on. Affirming my identity and solidarity with this tradition gives me my sense of being someone. Now when I talk with my mother I feel her strength, as I could not feel it earlier in my life. I see who she really is.

Still I remain the former fool who is healing but not yet healed. What is new is that I have found an inner peace. I feel at peace with the path I have walked. Of course, if I had been able to plan my path, I would not have planned it like that.

Now when I bring white people from Canada to the village, they are eager to meet my mother,. They treat her with a respect she deserves, but which my sophisticated, urban compatriots deny her in their supposed imitation of these white people. A further irony is that when these white visitors have shown interest in and respect for our food, culture, and village ways, my African intellectual friends have felt obliged to appreciate them also. Whereas the white people traumatized us and set us against ourselves through colonization, their recognition of the value of our culture may help bring us back to a sense of ourselves.

On a recent visit to Fienso, I brought an American woman student of mine. She came with a rich assortment of gifts, clothes for my mother, watches for the children. The other women in the family, who had detested me as a child, now wanted to claim credit for having nourished me and given me affection. They told my mother what a valuable child she had in me, what special friends I had. My friend brought medications and first aid treatments with her and helped the villagers. She gave a hundred dollars to my mother, which can go a long way in the village. To the villagers, the fact that my friend was American brought an additional sense of prestige to the village itself. The elders said, "American—that is even stronger than French. Now we have the power of the whites on our side."

Strangely, it was I, the good-for-nothing fool, Yaya, who was bringing white people to the village and helping to renew the people's sense of their own worth. How things can change!

At least the memory of Nangape has been preserved from disrespect. Now the people say he was truly a seer with a valid vision of things to come. If the reader were to go to Africa today to find a musician who specializes in healing through music, such as Nangape, a long search might prove futile. While dancing and music-making are practiced as uplifting activities—preventive therapy—the healing art is disappearing. New generations of Africans see the elder musicians as old-fashioned, and their arts are denigrated as charlatanism or sorcery. Belief in spirits and the invisible world are more and more seen as ancestral superstitions.

Students of Western medicine accept the long years of studying necessary to prepare them for their professional careers. Similarly, the Minianka musician-healers need lengthy training in musical technique, ritual, psychological understanding, and herbalism. Few young musicians show the patience for the long apprenticeship. Traditionally, each case must be approached individually. This does not correspond to the tendency in modern living to categorize and look for ready-made solutions. In playing music for a disturbed individual, the musician enters into a nonverbal communication with the unstated sources of the patient's problems. For the musical intervention to be effective, it must be an appropriate, spontaneous answer to the unpredictable responses of the patient. There is no way that the length of treatment required can be foreseen. It cannot fit into routine scheduling of office hours.

Africa has been affected by proponents of modern Western medicine who claim to have a monopoly on scientific knowledge. For many Africans, only medical doctors with diplomas have the right to speak about healing. They have resigned any faith in their traditions and believe in the white man's pills. As in other parts of the world, we may be witnessing in Africa today the disappearance of a large portion of the wealth of the human heritage. The old medical and musical traditions are falling into disuse. The elders die, and their knowledge dies with them.

The village orchestras I heard in my youth are gone. No one plays like them any more. The very musicians are lacking. Groups that had twenty candidates waiting for a chance to play when I was young have now fallen to one or two members only. The chances of doing serious healing work are diminishing—there are no longer musicians capable of serious accompaniment.

When I see the disappearance of this cultural wealth, when I see our initiation masks hanging in the museums of the West or even in our own national museums for the preservation of the cultural patrimony, I am saddened. The masks are meant to be worn, danced with, not hung on walls next to banal statements for tourists. The balafon had its place in the village; now it is incorporated into jazz groups in the West without any of its traditional significance. A xylophone could have served equally well but would not have looked as exotic. The elders who could instruct so well on the living meaning of the balafon sit unlistened to in the village square while Western professors explain in courses in music schools about the tonal and rhythmic structure of this "folk" music. I can say nothing to stop these transformations I see. Either the music is being destroyed, or all meaning is being taken out of it, or it is used blasphemously.

The star system I see in Western popular music goes very much against the standards of conduct for the village musician with which I was raised. The star does not give time to the community but to himself or herself. The star usually seeks to amaze people, not to care for them; to be admired and praised by the anonymous throngs, not to honor distinct individuals whose lives depend on one another in community. It is forgotten that the reason for playing is to bring well-being to people. This is different from driving fans into ecstasies of overexcitement. Music should not be a means to building a personal cult. That is idolatry. My village tradition teaches that music is a calling greater than the individual. I can give my life to it if I love it. In serving this music, I can share with other people and contribute to their joy and health.

In Africa today, youth no longer have a model to follow. Whatever hardships I may have suffered when I was young, I always had a model to follow in the elder, Nangape. I wanted to grow up to be like him. Once, his shirt had a hole burnt in it, so I burned mine in the same place. I wanted to be an orchestra leader like him, and I played this imaginary role. I saw myself turning around with the drum, speaking to the people, some of whom were in trance states, and singing and making others happy. I observed and learned all I could to become like my model.

Today the values have changed. There are no longer models such as those I had. The elders who stood for knowledge have been replaced by stars from outside our culture. The young dream of singing in a full auditorium, illuminated by bright lights, with lots of girls seeking autographs. Their ambition is to make a record that will sell widely. If they succeed, if they make millions, it is unlikely they will spend their time learning from an elder about how to care for people, about sacrificing themselves to play for fools who talk incomprehensibly. It is unlikely they will want to descend from the stage to play in a ceremony with its reputed spirits. The buildings and commercial products the West brought to Africa have not done as much harm as the lack of models.

Our elders were not able to foresee the cultural changes and their effects on the relations between the generations. When the white colonizers were in Africa, we danced in the village, they in their dance halls. When they left, we created forms of urban music such as the music called high life. With little new creativity, this is the popular music of today—the forms from this brief period of time are now considered classics. Meanwhile, the heritage of thousands of years is forgotten. The youth in the villages admire urban music, and the West imports it, saying it is real African music. The instruments, rhythms, harmonies, and melodies of hundreds of diverse ethnic groups with rich cultures are neglected. The nightclub music of the Westernized urban elites is claimed to be representative of whole nations.

I am struck with the irony of the situation that I witness in the West. People are seeking out the values of ancient traditions from many cultures because of what was lost in the materialistic advances of their secular culture. Can we in Africa not profit from this example? Do we have to lose everything of traditional value first before we set out to rediscover it? So many Westerners are satu- rated with all the material goods and conveniences possible, yet still they are unhappy. In Africa, the tendency is to want these very things that have failed to satisfy the people who possess them. We Africans do not know Westerners truly. Once we have killed our entire culture, will we have to reinvent it, or will we take it from elsewhere?

When I was six years old, I was already the leader of an orchestra of ten boys. Although this memory gives me a good laugh today, I realize how far African children now are from dreaming such dreams of growing up to be like the traditional elders.

It is up to everyone involved to reflect on what we want for our African future. At present, so many of us refuse to live the ways that have nourished us. After twenty years of living in Canada, I still do not understand the Western model that was proposed to us as the superior alternative to our traditions. How much less must those who remain in Africa understand it. The musicians among them dream of playing at the Olympia in Paris, or in New York, where they imagine there are no poor people.

A question perturbs me. Even if I communicate well about the traditions as I understand them, if I focus my interest on them, teach about them at the university in Canada, play the music itself—what model do I myself give? Is it the model of the traditional musician? Alas, the fact that I do these things in America only further encourages the young who become aware of me to want to come here themselves.

My mentor and protector, Nangape Kone, foresaw success in music for me and that I would be a man of knowledge. I am eager to discover just what knowledge is. Nangape himself exemplified for me all the best of human qualities: he was a guardian and transmitter of knowledge and of precious traditions.

In my youth he taught me some music, which I later recorded on the album named for him. Now it is played widely across North America. This means the knowledge it contains is being transmitted still. My role has been to pass on this music. An example will serve to show how I have done this.

My first record was played for a group of elders assembled by the Ministry of Culture to help preserve the Malian cultural patrimony. They are traditional practitioners who are in tune with the modern world. One selection had the same title as the record itself, "Nangape." As they listened to it, one of the elder musicians said, "Stop. Let's hear that again. The person who is playing that passage has knowledge in his hands." They listened to it repeatedly over the course of a week. The passage that had stirred the elders' interest so much cannot be described but is felt to lift all the music to another level.

I was brought before the elders. They looked at my hand and asked me all sorts of questions, such as who my grandfather was, where I came from, in what environment I had lived. I explained that I had lived in a mystical milieu, had played accompaniments at burials and funerals, and had been at many ceremonies of the secret societies.

That background was the source of the feeling they had that there was something in the hand of the man who was playing. This is not anything tangible. It had nothing to do with techniques of playing or with the material out of which the instruments were made. It was a feeling of knowledge that had slipped into the playing because it had been directly transmitted to me through repeated exposure over a long period of time. I assimilated it unconsciously; I was steeped in it. There can be no shortcuts to this knowledge, no technique-based appropriation of it, no institutionalized courses to give formal instruction in it. It is part of a living musical tradition, inseparable from the lives of the people in their most intense and meaningful moments of mystery. When you are sincerely playing the drums to celebrate and honor a man or a woman you have known for years, who has lived a good life and died, you are in touch with very deep currents of reality. You drum your knowledge as your fellow villagers dance it. The music emanates the truth you feel and know.

When I took up the drum and balafon again as an adult in Canada, in all solitude and with no guarantees of recognition, I assumed responsibility for the African legacy of my origins. This reconciled me with myself, my mother, my past, my destiny. I have never since found cause to doubt what I was taught as a child, that each instrument is a universe to be discovered each day throughout life. When I have said in workshops that the drum is the psychiatrist of my culture, I have not been joking. I continue to experience in my own life the ancestral wisdom of the healing drum.

PRONUNCIATION KEY AND GLOSSARY OF MINIANKA NAMES AND TERMS

bafoko (bah-fo-ko)   a hand drum made of a large calabash with a goatskin head

balafon (bah-lah-foan)   a wooden xylophone with gourd resonators

bolon (bow-loan)   a bass string instrument with a calabash resonator covered with goat skin, which is pierced by a millet stalk to which two strings are attached

bouu (boo)   family

coredjouga (ko-ray-joo-gah)   literally, scavenger; figuratively, a person with no need for material possessions

diomon (dee-oh-moan)   word

djémé (jem-bay)   a vase-shaped, wooden hand drum with a goatskin head

djinambori (gee-nam-bo-ree)   people who can perform extraordinary feats through the spirits they possess

dounouba (doo-noo-bah)   a Minianka dance to bring chronic conflicts to a head

dya (dee-ah)   shadow, double, an invisible aspect of the human being

fiaga (fee-ah-gah)   silence

Fienso (fee-en-so)   Yaya Diallo's native village

fourou (foo-roo)   marriage

hooro (hoe-roh)   dance

hoou (hoo)   death

PRONUNCIATION KEY AND GLOSSARY

kata (kah-tah) holiday

Kle (clay) God, the Creator

Kle-goa (clay-go-ah) House of God, a temple dedicated to Kle

Kle-kolo (clay-ko-lo) a system of rules laid out by Kle (the Creator) to maintain peace and balance in the community and the world as a whole

Komo (co-mo) one of the secret societies

Maniah (ma-nee-ah) the warrior's secret society

minan (mee-nan) nose, breath, the vital principle

nampou (nahm-poo) foreigner

Nangape (Nahn-gah-pay) the name of Yaya Diallo's music teacher and mentor

nanyaraga (nahn-yah-rah-gah) a predatory animal

n'bade (en-bah-day) a sibling from the same biological mother

n'fade (en-fah-day) a sibling from the same biological father but a different mother

n'fougon (en-foo-gon) the interior aspect of the human being with moral qualities

Nia (nee-ah) one of the secret societies

Niewoh (nee-ay-wo) a woman's secret society

n'kere (en-kay-ray) the physical body of the human being

n'kie (en-key-ay) the whole of knowledge available in the cosmos

nou (noo) mother

n'peenyee (en-pain-yay) a long, wooden drum with goatskin on each end; it is hit with a stick

n'pia (en-pee-ah) child

n'tio (en-tee-oh) father

nyama (nee-ya-ma) various meanings: remorse, a malefic power from a murdered person or animal, or the soul of a murdered being that haunts the killer

sara (sah-rah) tobacco

sicanfolo (see-cahn-fo-lo) a sorcerer with harmful intent; poisoner

sigue-chim (see-gay-cheem) inhabitants of the bush, spirits

Sikasso (see-kah-so) a city in Mali

sikiere-folo (see-key-ay-ray-foe-low) a person who is behaving bizarrely, showing emotional or mental disturbance

soume (soo-may) an alcoholic drink derived from honey

tama (tah-mah) an hourglass-shaped hand drum, carved of wood and covered on both ends by lizard skin

tien (tee-en) heritage, inheritance

tipia (tee-pee-ah) human being

PRONUNCIATION KEY AND GLOSSARY

wa ti pinkie (wah-tee-pin-kee-ay)   someone knowledgeable about human behavior, philosophy, sociology

wa weree nkie (wah-weh-ray-en-kee-ay)   someone knowledgeable about medicinal herbs

weree (weh-ray)   sum of individual and community knowledge about healing, including knowledge of the use of fetishes to protect against dangers

wogne n'kiefolo (wohn-yay-en-kee-fo-lo)   seer, soothsayer

yatinyi (yah-teen-yee)   musical instruments

y siri durouta fla burouta   proverb: if you want to have a chief, start a bad habit

Zangasso (zahn-ga-so)   the village where Yaya Diallo's mother was born

SELECTED
BIBLIOGRAPHY

Bastien, Christine. *Folies, mythes et magies d'Afrique: Propos de guérrisseurs du Mali.* Paris: Editions L'Harmattan, 1988.

Bebey, Francis. *African Music—A People's Art.* Westport: Lawrence Hill and Company, 1979.

Bentov, Itzhak. *Stalking the Wild Pendulum.* Rochester, Vermont: Destiny Books, 1988.

Berendt, Joachim-Ernst. *Nada Brahma: The World Is Sound.* Rochester, Vermont: Destiny Books, 1987.

Bohannan, Paul. *Africa and Africans.* Garden City, New York: Natural History Press, 1964.

Chernoff, John Miller. *African Rhythm and African Sensibility: Aesthetics and Social Action in African Musical Idioms.* Chicago: University of Chicago Press, 1979.

Colleyn, Jean-Paul and Danielle Jonckers. "Ceux qui refusent le maître: La conception du pouvoir chez les minyanka du Mali," *Africa* (53)4, 1983.

Diallo, Yaya. *Profil culturel Africain.* Montreal: Centre Interculturel Monchanin, 1985.

Fage, J. D. *A History of Africa.* New York: Alfred A. Knopf, 1979.

Gibbal, J. M. *Tambours d'eau: Sanghais, Soninke, Malinke.* Paris: Editions le Sycomore, 1982.

Holas, Bohumil. *Les Senoufo, y compris les Minianka.* Paris: Presses Universitaires de France, 1957.

Imperato, Pascal J. *Historical Dictionary of Mali,* 2nd edition. Metuchen, New Jersey: Scarecrow Press, 1986.

SELECTED BIBLIOGRAPHY

Imperato, Pascal J. and Eleanor M. Imperato. *Mali: A Handbook of Historical Statistics*. Boston: G. K. Hall, 1982.

Jaynes, Julian. *The Origin of Consciousness in the Breakdown of the Bicameral Mind*. Boston: Houghton Mifflin, 1976.

Jonckers, Danielle. *La société Minianka du Mali*. Paris: Editions L'Harmattan, 1987.

Knight, Roderic. "African Music," *Academic American Encyclopedia*, vol. 1, pp. 168–171. Danbury, Connecticut: Grolier, 1984.

Kotchy, D. Nguessan. "Fonction sociale de la musique traditionnelle," *Présence Africaine* 93, 1975.

Murchie, Guy. *The Seven Mysteries of Life*. Boston: Houghton Mifflin, 1978.

Ostrander, Sheila and Lynn Schroeder. *Superlearning*. New York: Dell, 1979.

Roberts, Richard L. *Warriors, Merchants, and Slaves: The State and the Economy in the Middle Niger Valley, 1700 to 1914*. Stanford, California: Stanford University Press, 1987.

Tomatis, Alfred A. *La nuit uterine*. Paris: Editions Stock, 1981.

Tompkins, Peter and Christopher Bird. *The Secret Life of Plants*. New York: Harper & Row, 1973.

Thompson, Robert Ferris. *Flash of the Spirit: African & Afro-American Art & Philosophy*. New York: Random House, 1984.

Verny, Thomas with John Kelly. *The Secret Life of the Unborn Child*. New York: Summit Books, 1981.

INDEX

Adults, age groups, 40–41
Age groups
    in restoring health, 156
    village, 38–41
Agriculture, Mali, 7
Alcoholic drinks, 30–31
Alize, 7
Ancestors, 13–15, 25
    ceremony of, 166–69
    disturbances by, 155–56
    stone of, 20
    worship of, 59–60
Animists, 9, 11, 24
    and spirits, 61–62
Apprentice, 95–97
Arrows, poison, 32–33
Artisans, 42
Ascariasis, 33
Assimilation, 179–81
Avocados, teacher's vs. farmer's way to
    grow, 121–23

Bafoko, 91–92
Bakari Oulougueme, 32–33

Balafon, 3, 5, 34, 48, 90–91, 108–9
Ballet companies, 114
Batrou Sekou, 108
Beatings by schoolteachers, 130
Beings of bush, spirits as, 156–59
Bolon, 91–92, 108
Bon-yi, 137
Boys, age groups, 38–39
Breakdancing, 178–79

Cadence magazine, 189
Calabash, and drinking, 30–31
Canada
    becoming chemist in, 183–85
    scholarship to, 181–83
Carleton University, 5
Cattle herders, 42
    dance, 112, 113
Cauvin, Jean, 9
Celebrations, 30
Ceremony
    of ancestors, 166–69
    Nia society, 133–35
Chemist, in Canada, 183–85

INDEX

Children, 28–29
Circle, 114
Circumcision, 64–66
  dance, 110
Climate, Mali, 7
Clitoris, excision, 39–40, 70
Communal life, 38–41
Coredjouga, 177–79
Crops, Mali, 7
Customs, 29–31

Daba, 106–7, 112
Daily life, and music, 107–9
Dance, 109–11
  occupational, 112–13
  of personality, 113–15
  stick, 111
  and work, 105–6, 112–13
Dancers
  Komo, 68–69
  and musicians, 98–99, 110–11
Dancing
  magico-religious, 110
  and music, 80–81
  observation of, 99–100
Death, 59–60
Democratic Union of the Malian
  People, 6
Diabate, Sidiki, 108
Diagnosis of illness, 150–53
Diomon, and fiaga, 58
Disturbances, by ancestors, 155–56
Divination, 154
Djémé, 3, 5, 92–93
Djinambori, 143
Double, 55–56
Dounouba, 111
Downbeat magazine, 189
Dreams, 153–54
Drums, 48–49, 107–8
  djémé, 92–93
  and healing, 161
  tama, 93–94
Dry season, Mali, 7
Dya, 55

Education, girls, 39–40
Egalitarianism, 37–38
Ego, and music, 102–4
Elders, 25–26, 44–47
  Nangape Kone, 47–51
Emotional disturbance, and music, 82–83

Epilepsy, 153
Evil spirits, 60–61
Excision, clitoris, 39–40, 70

Family, 25–29
  customs, 29–31
  in Fienso, 19–20
  herding and music, 33–36
  inheritance, 31–32
Farmers, 41
Fathers, 26–27
Festival
  Maniah, 131–32
  Niewoh, 70–71
Fetish, 52–53
  Maniah festival, 131–32
  Nia ceremony, 134
Fiaga, and diomon, 58
Fienso, 10–11, 17–20
Filariasis, 153
Fire initiation, 67
Firstborn tree, 20–21
Fishermen, 41
Folktales, about hunter of souls, 147–49
Foreigners, 29–30
Fourou, 27
Fruits, Mali, 8
Fulani, 11, 13–14, 42
Funerals, 135–40
Funerary dances, 110

Gamma Zero, 173–77
Gates, family compound, 20
Genealogy, and music, 101
Geomancy, 62–63
Gifts, offered by guests, 30
Girls
  age groups, 39–40
  and healing drum, 163–66
Glossolalia, 84
Gomba, 110
Government, Mali, 8
Guests, gifts offered by, 30

Harmattan wind, 7
Harvest dance, 112
Healers, musicians as, 150–53, 162–63
Healing, 54–55
  and music, 101–2, 159–62
Healing drum, 198–99
  recordings of, 188–89
  and young girl, 163–66

INDEX

Health
  and music, 82–83
  restoring, 156
Herders, 42
Herding, and music, 33–36
Heritage, 13–15
Hernia, Nangape and, 143–45
Hoeing dance, 112
Holidays, 30
Hooro, 109
Hoou, 59–60
Houyees, 59
Human beings, 55–57
  effects of sound on, 97–98
Hunters, 41–42
  dances, 112–13
  Naho secret society, 69–70
  of souls, 147–49, 170–71

Illness
  diagnosis, 150–53
  treatment, 149–50
Inheritance, 31–32
Initiation
  circumcision, 64–66
  dances, 109–10
  fire, 67
  girls, 39–40
Interior, 56–57
Islam, spread of, 23, 190–92

Kantey, Sumanguru, 91
Karite, 8
Kata, 30
Kle, 52–53
Kle-goa, 53
Kle-kolo, 53, 79
Komo secret society, 68–69, 132–33
Kone, Mansha, 33, 35
Kone, Nangape. See Nangape Kone

Languages
  Africa, 5
  Mali, 9–10
  of spirits, 60
Lenin Prize, 181
Life threat, 142–43
Lion hunter's dance, 110

Madness, slow, 169–70
Magico-religious dances, 110
Mali, 6–10
  return to, 189–90

spread of Islam in, 190–92
Mali Center for Rehabilitation, 189
Mali Federation, 6
Maniah festival, 131–32
Maniah secret society, 73–74
Mansha Kone, 33, 35
Marriage, 27–28
Memory, and music, 100 101
Men, Nia secret society, 72–73
Mental illness, 150–53
Minan, 55–56
Monotony, and healing, 160–61
Montreal, University of, 4, 183, 184
Mother(s), 27, 31–32, 54–55, 193–95
  circle of, 26
  as coredjouga, 177–79
Music, 79–80
  and daily life, 107–9
  and dancing, 80–81
  effects of sound, 97–98
  and ego, 102–4
  for funeral, 136–37
  and healing, 101–2, 159–62
  and health, 82–83
  and herding, 33–36
  lessons from Nangape Kone, 48–51
  and memory, 100–101
  proverbs about, 37
  teacher, 95–97
  women and, 81–82
  and work, 41–42, 106–7
Musical instruments, 86–90
  bafoko, 91–92
  balafon, 90–91
  bolon, 91–92
  djémé, 92–93
  initiation, 66
  rhythms, 94
  of secret societies, 75
  tama, 93–94
Musician(s)
  apprentice, 95–96
  and dancers, 98–99, 110–11
  as healers, 150–53, 162–63, 195–96
  Komo, 68–69
  observation of, 100

Naho secret society, 69–70
Nampou, 29–30
Nangape Kone, 4, 47–51, 88–89, 95, 104,
  123, 126–28, 163, 195, 197, 198
  and hernia, 143–45

INDEX

Nangape (recording), 4, 189, 198–99
Nanyaraga, 56
Native American dances, 116–17
Natural world, 24
N'bade, 29
Neighborhoods, in Fienso, 18–19
N'fade, 29
N'fougon, 56
Nia secret society, 72–73, 142
    ceremony, 133–35
Niewoh secret society, 70–72
Niger River, 6
N'kere, 55
N'kie, 54
N'peenyee drums, 48–49, 89
N'pia, 28–29
N'Yago, 51
Nyama, 169–70

Observation
    of dancing, 99–100
    of musicians, 100
Occupational dances, 112–13
Orchestra, 80, 88, 96, 110–11
Oulougueme, Bakari, 32–33

Personality, dance of, 113–15
Poison arrows, 32–33
Population
    Africa, 5
    Mali, 6
Poro society, 142
Potters, 42
Prophecy, 15–17
Proverbs, about music, 37
Punishment, in school, 130

Recordings, 198–99
    of healing drum, 188–89
Regulation, by secret societies, 74–76
Religion, Mali, 9, 10, 23, 190–92
Retreat, initiation, 66
Rhythms, 94
Rituals, 24
    funeral, 135–40
    Maniah, 131–32
Round of seasons, 110
Rummaging spirit, possession by, 151

Sacred wood, 20–24
    and conversion to Islam, 23
Sacrifices, 21–22, 53, 73

Sankore, University of, 6
Sara, 30
Saxaphone, 5
Scholarship, 123–26
    to Canada, 181–83
School
    and assimilation, 179–81
    colonial teachers, 119–21
    high school boarder, 172–73
    and label of Gamma Zero, 173–77
    and scholarship, 123–26, 181–83
    and teacher's vs. farmer's way to grow
        avocados, 121–23
Secret societies
    Komo, 68–69
    Maniah, 73–74
    Naho, 69–70
    Nia, 72–73
    Niewoh, 70–72
    social regulation by, 74–76
Secular dances, 109
Seer, 54
Sekou, Batrou, 108
Sexual orientation, and dancing, 99
Sicanfolo, 60–61
Sidiki Diabate, 108
Sigue-chim, 60
Sikiere-folo, 146–47, 150–53
Silence, and word, 58
Slow madness, 169–70
Smiths, 42
Social regulation, by secret
        societies, 74–76
Sorcerers, 42, 54, 60–61
Souls, 56
    hunter of, 170–71
Soume, 30
Sound, effects of, 97–98
Sowing dance, 112
Spirits, 60–62, 154–55
    as beings of bush, 156–59
Stick dances, 111
Stone of ancestors, 20
Sumanguru Kantey, 91

Taboos, in Fienso, 17
Tama, 93–94
Teacher
    colonial, 119–21
    mother as, 27
    of music, 95–97
Telli, 26, 178–79

INDEX

Tien, 31–32
Tipia, 55–57
Tobacco, 30
Trance, 83–85, 115–18
  Komo society, 132–33
  Maniah festival, 131–32
  Nia ceremony, 134–35
Trees, Mali, 7
Tree spirits, 61

Veterinarians, 42
Village
  cleansing after chief dies, 138–40
  conversion to Islam, 23
Village life, 10, 37–38
  age groups, 38–41
  work, 41–43
Violin, 5

Warriors, Maniah secret society, 73–74

Water, as vital principle, 24
Water drum, 81–82
Water spirits, 61
Weree, 54–55
Westernization, in high school, 172–77
Wildlife, Mali, 7
Wogne n'kiefolo, 54
Women
  circle of, 26
  and music, 81–82
  Niewoh secret society, 70–72
Wood, sacred, 20–24
Word, and silence, 58
Work, 41–43
  and dance, 105–6, 112–13
  and music, 106–7

Yatinyi, 89–90

Zangasso, 8, 14, 21, 22–23

ABOUT THE AUTHORS

Yaya Diallo was trained on balafon and hand drums by his grandfather and by his spiritual mentor, Nangape. Although he now lives in Montreal and teaches and performs drumming internationally, he returns frequently to his home in Mali to renew his ties with the elders. Seeing the teachings he grew up with gradually being lost to Westernization in his native country, he encourages the youth of his village to take pride in their cultural heritage. Yaya's most recent audiocassette recording, **The Healing Drum,** features the traditional and ceremonial music described in this book.

Mitchell Hall received his degree in comparative religions from Columbia University and in sociology from the University of Chicago. He joined the Peace Corps as a volunteer teacher in West Africa, where his love for African music and dance was instilled. Since his return to the United States, Mitch has worked as a professional writer, translator, teacher, and health therapist. It was through their common interest in African culture that Mitch and Yaya met, embarking on a long-term friendship and collaboration.

THE HEALING DRUM AUDIOCASSETTE

African Ceremonial and Healing Music

By Yaya Diallo

Yaya Diallo plays sacred and celebratory rhythms of the Minianka tribe on traditional African instruments, such as the djémé hand drum, balafon, and tama (talking drum). Included are on-sight recordings of ceremonial and ritual music from Yaya's home in Mali, West Africa, and new recordings of traditional rhythms played and sung by Yaya and accompanists.

Each selection is an authentic representation of Minianka musical culture, including healing rhythms of the water drum, music for community circle dances, drumming to honor a chief and to precede the planting season, and music of the secret societies.

Yaya Diallo has performed and taught hand drums, dance, and songs of the Minianka, Malinke, Lobi, and Senufo people throughout the United States and Canada. He lives and teaches in Montreal.

40-minute audiocassette, $9.95
Available at many fine bookstores or, to order direct, send a check or money order for the total amount, plus $2.00 shipping and handling for the first tape and $1.00 for each additional tape to:

> Inner Traditions International
> One Park Street
> Rochester, Vermont 05767

A complete catalog of books from Inner Traditions is available upon request from the above address.